GLP
Greenwich Leadership Partners

CREATING SCHOOLS THAT THRIVE

A BLUEPRINT FOR STRATEGY

STEPHANIE ROGEN

Founder, Greenwich Leadership Partners

Cover and Interior Design by Creative Roam, www.creativeroam.com

First Printing, 2018

ISBN 978-0-692-12970-8

Greenwich Leadership Partners
PO Box 324
Old Greenwich, CT 06870

www.greenwichleadershippartners.com

ACKNOWLEDGMENTS

Writing a book is a truly collaborative endeavor, and I could not have accomplished it without the contributions of countless school communities, friends, and colleagues. I'd like to offer special thanks to everyone at Greenwich Leadership Partners for the encouragement and support from the moment I began talking about this project. I'd also like to express my deepest appreciation to my reading and writing collaborators Charlie Gofen, Kirk Greer, Pamela Liflander, and Rob Riordan. I could not have written this book without you. Special thanks also to Tony Wagner and Ted Dintersmith, who encouraged me to write, provided mentorship, and offered invaluable advice along the way.

Finally, I'd like to thank my family: Gerry, Will, Christa, and Julia. Where I see limitations, you see the possibilities. I love you!

PREFACE

How to Use this Book

Creating Schools That Thrive: A Blueprint for Strategy is a working guide for your school's strategic design process. While I offer case studies from my partnerships with independent schools, my experience working with public schools also affirms that my approach to strategic design and my reflections on how to effectively manage change are relevant to any school community.

I suggest that you read through the whole book before doing the exercises. Once you've gotten a sense of the bigger picture, you'll be ready to make the content of this book work best for your school. Feel free to use the book like a workbook, one that you can return to again and again. There is lots of space to write down your questions, your observations, and your reflections.

As you document what you've learned and understand how these exercises work best for your school, you'll build a working knowledge for strategic design. Think of this book as a facilitator's guide that you can reference and update. The GLP website (www.greenwichleadershippartners.com) has additional downloadable templates to support all of the exercises found in this book.

TABLE OF CONTENTS

INTRODUCTION: STRATEGIC DESIGN IS THE ROUTE TO CHANGE

School leaders and Board members often come to me with their concerns about educating students in an age that is being reshaped by automation, machine learning, and globalization. They worry about the relevance and sustainability of their schools. Savvy educators and parents know that today's children, and the generations that come after them, will face real-world challenges arising from profound economic and cultural disruptions that are changing the way we live, work, and learn. Schools want to change. Schools need to change! The challenge is how, and schools are now looking to strategy and planning as a means to that end. I wrote this book because I've discovered that schools need concrete tools and methods to design and implement strategy. If schools can act strategically, they will not only adapt and stay relevant but be extraordinary.

I did not write this book to make the case for change in our schools. Many others have done that well, with stories and data and research that compel us to rethink school. My goal with this book is to tackle the related question—*how to change*. I've found that the transition from why to how is the most challenging piece of the puzzle.

The questions of *what to change* and *how to change* are going to vary from school community to school community. Some schools may not yet know where they are in relationship to future needs; others may know what they want, or even what they need, but are not sure how to go about it. In every school, there will be questions regarding how quickly to move, how radically to reinvent, and how to ensure all children succeed.

I HEAR THE RIGHT QUESTIONS FROM EDUCATORS DAILY:

» **What knowledge, skills, and dispositions do young people need to thrive, now and in the future?**

» **What is the optimal environment for developing these skills and dispositions?**

» **How do we facilitate and assess those outcomes?**

» **How do we create the conditions and culture that are best for our learners?**

» **How do we create schools where kids are healthy and able to thrive beyond college placement?**

» **How do we change as teachers and educators? How do we develop new capacities and skills as we educate our students?**

» **How do we engage with our communities so that we can effectively change?**

» **How do we learn to design and execute strategies that will drive these changes without intolerable risk to our children or the school's bottom line?**

Strategic design is not so different from good, inquiry-based learning—and at Greenwich Leadership Partners (GLP) that's exactly how I teach schools to do the work. I know that strategy designed to answer questions like the ones above requires real change—and change is messy. As an educator, you know that learning is not necessarily linear, and most often it's experiential. You also know learning requires feedback. It requires revision and rework. And, it requires both discipline and agility in order to make progress.

All these ideas are embedded in GLP's approach. By using this book as your guide, you will not design a long and detailed strategic plan to be perfected on paper, and then handed down so folks in your school can execute it. Your team will perceive that to-do list as a burden. Instead, you're going to craft a vision, make a few overarching choices, and then allow your people to get to work: you'll rapidly adjust and adapt throughout the process, using the plan as a high-level, flexible road map rather than a comprehensive, step-by-step process that may or may not yield the results you want.

Strategy is by its very nature a learning experience, and I believe that what you learn through doing this work will translate to a new understanding of learning in the classroom. Conversely, what you do with students has immediate application to strategy. One of my primary goals is to help you develop a great pedagogy for learning deeply about your own school and its future. Just as your students do when your school is at its best, you will experience great learning and then use it to transform your organization. Ultimately, you will be creating the best learning environment for your students—and your adults. Welcome to the strategic design process!

Strategy or Planning?

When I began my consulting work with schools, it became immediately evident that my clients' understanding of strategy was completely different from my experiences with it in both the for-profit and nonprofit sectors. My first day working with a New Jersey boarding school was telling. Chan Hardwick, then the Headmaster for twenty-two years at Blair Academy, met me in his office at the encouragement of my former boss and his Trustee, Donald McCree. Chan was skeptical about consultants, and even more skeptical about strategic planning. After a polite greeting he made his position clear. A tall and commanding presence, he looked at me with eyebrows arched and said, "Stephanie, do you want to know what I really think about strategic planning?"

I'm not sure he waited for my reply. He simply leaned over behind his desk and began shuffling through drawers to pull out a neatly bound sheaf of papers that he slapped down on his desk with contempt: "This endless list of stuff is what I think of it!"

Chan was illustrating what I learned would be true for many schools. Strategic planning didn't engage community members in deep reflection about the purpose of the school or the experience of its students in relation to its context. All it did was catalogue a list of ongoing activities the school would have taken on anyway. Alternatively, the plan was a lot of lofty and aspirational language more likely designed for marketing purposes to better describe the school. But as a call to action, the plan was relatively useless, merely collecting dust instead of capturing and directing the attention of the school's stakeholders.

Schools use the word *strategy*, but most often they are actually talking about *business planning*, or worse, *business-as-usual planning*. Typically, schools work within an artificial construct, called a "strategic planning cycle" tied to accreditation or in anticipation of a new campaign. Every five years or so, schools will create a committee, craft a wish list of new ideas and options, superficially check in with their constituents, and then lay out a plan that states what they hope to accomplish.

How many times have you read a school plan that says it will recruit the best faculty possible; offer excellent academics; ensure a strong endowment and great facilities; and offer some type of programming that aligns with a current educational trend? The "how" of these kinds of plans is limited to the typical activities of any school: it might include supporting and reviewing faculty and staff, assessing academic offerings and reviewing curriculum, making sure that facilities are up to snuff, and reviewing the accounting ledgers to meet fiscally responsible mandates. Occasionally, there is a commitment to add a new offering. Then the plan will be translated into a lofty marketing piece with a proud letter from the Board and Head of School that articulates a grand and rosy vision for the future. Yet the truth is, this new plan looks essentially like that of any other school.

Let's be clear: these types of plans outline what every school should be doing all the time. They are worthy to-do lists, but they are merely the table stakes for healthy functioning schools. The plans—and those who lead the development of these plans—do not address the coherent and compelling choices the school makes to achieve a distinctive position and create the best conditions for the success of *their* students.

What if schools could not only improve business as usual, but sharpen understanding of who they are and how they could better serve their communities? What if schools could move beyond plans that feel static to designs that are dynamic, visible, and living elements of day-to-day life at that school? What if schools could make better choices, choices that reflect a clear sense of mission and values? What if systematic change could be made without sacrificing student outcomes, breaking budgets, or creating havoc? What if the strategic plan moved from being a "plan in the drawer" to driving the way we work, learn, and operate every day?

Well, it can. In my experience at GLP, these are the expected outcomes of real strategic planning.

Since 2010, GLP has facilitated change and supported leadership and governance for more than 64 independent schools and school districts, as well as higher education organizations and education-based not-for-profits. I believe that the GLP process speaks to what schools want most: the opportunity to design a strategy that actualizes a compelling sense of purpose and a clear and unique value proposition for their families. Schools come away with a new understanding of how they do what they do, why it's valuable, and who they want to serve.

The good news is that you, in whatever context, can adapt universal elements of the GLP process for your school. My approach to strategic design is descriptive, rather than prescriptive, so it is easily adapted in any circumstance and for any community. All you need is a strong desire to take on the work. If you are ready, my philosophy of strategy, design, and implementation works because it tests your existing structures and assumptions, thereby unleashing the talent and knowledge within your system. You'll be amazed at what you can do with the resources you have!

Schools Need to Think Differently About Change

When I was in graduate school studying how organizations change, I became acquainted with the work of Peter Senge, Ron Heifetz, and John Kotter, all of whom were talking and writing about how organizations learn. What became clear to me was that the most adaptive and resilient organizations, in any context or industry, are those that thrive because the adults within them are learning effectively, all the time. So when I started my consulting business, I assumed that schools—which are all about learning—would operate better, like the best organizations in any industry. I was shocked to learn that the truth for most schools seems to be far from that ideal.

Many schools are organized as fairly traditional structures with deeply embedded and long-standing ways of operating that leave adults isolated, with limited space or time for authentic collaboration. Formal administrative leadership roles are often organized in "silos" (vertical stand alone functions), part-time smaller "leadership titles" abound, and meeting and committee structures describe how collective work is supposed to happen. The design of organization, space, and time in the lives of teachers and administrators leaves little room for authentic teaming, and limited or no cross-functional collaboration. Schools are simply not organized to empower faculty and staff to research, design and incubate new practices as a way to solve problems and improve learning. Organic leadership is usually the result of an "outlier," someone inside or outside the organization, who has the rare combination of savvy and influence to mobilize others and spread new ideas and practices.

Most professional development and professional learning I've encountered reflects the practice of industry thirty to forty years ago and is detached from the real work of school. Adult learning often means attending a workshop for a day and trying out some new tricks with the students, or hearing a speaker and experimenting in workshop format. Teachers then go back to their classrooms, may or may not test new practices, and often have little opportunity to share their learning and expertise in a collaborative and consistent way. As a result, it's difficult to scale or spread new ideas or practices inside the school—even though we can attest new things are happening in the corners of almost every school! If you are learning in a school that operates this way, how can we expect our children to learn differently?

Schools need to think more strategically about what it means to learn—not just for children but also for adults. How do we best develop and nurture our collective talents? How can schools design an organization that reflects this commitment and frees adults to continually grow and adapt to the needs of all learners—adult and child? These are the questions that allow me to engage school leaders.

I believe that schools would benefit from lessons learned in other industries and organizations, especially those that have clear, deeply-held values. When you think about the most successful companies today, whether they're big global conglomerates or entrepreneurial startups, they all share a passion for innovation—for incubating new ways of doing things—and they all have deeply-held, unifying values that determine how they work. They are flexible in the ways they operate and their leadership supports the conditions for the right talent to flourish. These organizations design backwards from, and in collaboration with, their users, whether patients, consumers, or clients. Think of organizations like the Mayo Clinic, Google, IBM, Netflix, or stalwarts like PepsiCo/Frito-Lay as just a few examples of businesses that learn, test, and evolve.

Because I've worked in both school and corporate environments, I bring a useful blend of insights to my clients. I help schools learn and adopt the best practices of the corporate world, particularly when it comes to creating strategy and implementing change. While the origin of strategic design consulting lies in enhancing corporate management practices, many of the approaches are valuable in helping schools deliver on their noble missions and respond with purpose to the radically changing context for schools in the twenty-first century.

How I Came to This Work

My work integrates more than twenty-five years of experience in the corporate, educational, and not-for-profit sectors. But before I accomplished anything on my resumé, I was the child who loved school. School has always been my safe haven. When I was young my family moved often, and the classroom—whatever town or country it was located in—was always the one place where I felt at home. I connected with learning, and I connected with teachers. I always imagined that I'd have a career in which I could be in schools—but the idea of teaching just didn't feel right. I realized that what I loved about school was more about the relationships and the qualities of the learning experiences. By the time I was in college, I knew that I wanted to be in a collaborative environment where I could continue learning, but where I could also work with and learn from adults.

After college I chose a job that promised learning: a year-long training program at the First National Bank of Boston. It was a good instinct and, in hindsight, a choice that shaped my thinking about adult learning and leadership. I spent the next several years in banking, ultimately transitioning from learning to be a banker to helping other bankers become better communicators, better relationship managers, and better problem solvers. I became a teacher, but by a different route. Of course I didn't make that connection then—I simply wore the title of consultant.

But I still yearned for work that involved schools. I didn't know what I would need to get there so I did what many of us do: I went back to school. I applied to the Harvard Graduate School of Education, was accepted into the Master's program, and naively proposed that I design my own curriculum. I would spend a third of my graduate studies at the Harvard Business School, a third at the Kennedy School of Government, and a third at the School of Education. At first my request was met with some surprise (actually more like shock). But I was granted the opportunity I created, and I leapt at the chance. I studied with the top people in each of their fields: experts like Ron Heifetz and Jim Sebenius at the Kennedy School; David Kuechle and Susan Moore Johnson at the Ed School, and disciples of Michael Porter at the Business School. All of these people offered me different lenses on how to lead and manage change in organizations.

My graduate studies were exhilarating, but the credentials I gained weren't enough to land me a job working with schools. Even though my degree was a Master's in Education with a focus in Administration and Policy, I hadn't come up through the traditional routes, and I had never been a teacher. Schools couldn't figure out what to do with me—where did I belong? I ended up right back on Wall Street working in, you guessed it, a bank.

This time, I got a job working closely with a CEO and former client who was completely redesigning an international bank that had been recently acquired. He knew this position was his last major banking job, and needed to develop a succession plan. I found myself working at the intersection of leadership, strategy, and change. I started to compile my own observations about how adults learn in organizations, how they adapt and react to change, and how they lead in the face of new realities. I was hooked, but more than that, I saw exactly how I might make a difference in educational systems. I honed my skills and eventually transitioned into being an independent consultant focused on partnering with schools.

My first client was Columbia University, in 2010. The executive team that was charged with leading the design and construction of a brand new campus needed help. Columbia had taken over 25 square blocks in Upper West Harlem, and a beautiful new campus, still in progress to this day, will certainly be at the core of president Lee Bollinger's legacy. I reported to the Executive Vice President in charge of real estate, facilities, and student services for the entire university. I knew nothing about building a new campus, but I did know a lot about helping teams and helping adults learn how to function effectively within a new paradigm or a new situation. I understood how organizational design, structures, and systems can either clear the path for adults to do their work well or complicate their efforts.

My next client was Blair Academy, an independent boarding school in New Jersey. Blair Academy was run by a dynamic team, Chan Hardwick and his wife, Monie, who functioned as a development partner and became leader of the strategic planning process. I convinced them that perhaps there was a better way to do a strategy than printing out wish lists, and my way would actually advance their school. I also encouraged them to address the elephant in the room, which was that Chan and Monie were going to retire in the near future. This reality was essential context for their strategy. Once hired, I helped them think seriously about succession and craft a plan that made important choices designed to fortify the core values of the school, preparing it for transition when a new leader would take over and lead the school anew. In the end, the school was so taken by this new approach that they invited me to co-present our work at the annual conference for The Association for Boarding Schools.

I also continued to work in the for-profit space, with a focus on grooming millennial talent and leaders. My questions about the "gap" between K-18 education and changing workforce needs led me to a vibrant collaboration with Ted Dintersmith, Tony Wagner, and Greg Whiteley. Ted had a vision for a film that would provoke these kinds of questions and inspire meaningful dialogue. *Most Likely To Succeed* premiered at Sundance in January of 2015. I served on panels at community events and film festivals and I facilitated dialogues with parents, educators, and students. I learned what communities across the country were worried about and what they wanted for their children. The film has been viewed by thousands of educators, politicians, business leaders, and school communities, sparking conversations across the globe about the purpose and design of school.

My experiences have allowed me to learn about how schools work and learn. Today, GLP helps each client school find its unique answer to the essential question: "How are we going to create an environment where our learners succeed?" The answer will be found within the existing culture of your organization, and in the context in which you operate—for example, if you're a rural school in Appalachia, your students' needs may be different than if you're a school in Los Angeles. No matter where your starting point is, you'll discover new ways of thinking, doing, and learning that drive innovation and transformation!

The Strategic Design Process

A great strategic design empowers schools to make winning choices that are dynamic, clear, and firmly rooted in their school's values. This book outlines the same strategic design approach, tools, and exercises that I use with my clients. Whether you are a leader, a Trustee, a board member, or a teacher who hopes to support change in your school, the approach to designing strategy I offer in this book can help. My goal is to offer you more than inspiration: this book is a road map to follow. My hope is that you'll get what you need to lead an effective strategic design process. I'll teach you how to engage your community, facilitate dialogue, articulate your values, build a collective vision, and develop a strategy and value proposition that advances your mission and focuses your community. I will help you consider the tough choices you need to make in order to resist the trap of being all things for all people. You will learn how to create coherence, which happens when you align your values with how your school operates every day.

Design Thinking: A Way of Working

The lessons in the rest of the book are reflected in the process of design thinking, a methodical approach to listening deeply, solving problems, creating solutions, and inventing new products or processes that improve experiences. This process was developed by the global design company IDEO and has roots in the principles of design. I've used design thinking to help executive teams in the healthcare industry redesign their meeting and collaboration practices, or reimagine critical practices in service of patients. I have coached teachers to use design thinking to innovate ninth-grade transitions for new high school students, and to structure classroom research projects in ways that are both inventive and highly engaging for students. I've seen schools use design thinking to engage alumni and parents, Trustees and leaders, as they confront adaptive challenges, roadblocks, and new opportunities for improving their schools.

I like to think of design thinking as a way of working: a series of steps that focuses on the needs of users and fosters creativity and a commitment to a dynamic and iterative process. A design thinking approach encourages experimentation, rapid learning, and deep collaboration. It's fun, optimistic, and inclusive. You can tackle small challenges and large-scale problems. In schools, it has applications from the classroom to the boardroom, and, of course, in developing your strategy. It's a terrific way to transition from ethnographic research, visioning, and values identification to the question of "How do we operationalize these ideas?" You'll move from the hypotheses of the Board and leadership to testing the concrete implications of these ideas in your community.

Build Design Thinking Skills

There are five design thinking phases, but think of them as the methodologies of a flexible mindset that you can use in all phases of the work:

1. Empathize: Empathy is the centerpiece of the design process. In this mode, you will work to understand your colleagues, the ways they interpret community expectations, and the reasons why they behave or respond in particular ways. You'll listen without judgment, seeking only to understand. Empathy interviews are a way of doing your ethnographic work and help you develop a broader and deeper investigation into the practices and experiences you are hoping to better understand. You will uncover how your community thinks about the world and what is meaningful about your school. You will learn about the audience you are designing for (the students) through observations and interviews that allow you to engage with them in the context of their lives, so that you can share in their experience.

2. Define: The define mode brings clarity and focus to the design space. It is your chance and responsibility to define the challenge you are taking on, based on what you have learned about your users—your teachers, staff, parents, and students—and about the context in which your challenge exists. The define mindset part of the work is essential to making good choices—and with it you will continue to sharpen your choices. The goal of the define mode is to craft a point of view that is based on the insights shared during the empathy work. In this case, you will "define" by revising a one-page statement of your strategy and creating a new version that reflects what you've learned.

3. Ideate: Ideate is the mode of the design thinking process in which you concentrate on idea generation. It represents brainstorming "going wide": imagining concepts, tactics, and outcomes in a collaborative, unfiltered setting. Ideation provides both the fuel and the source material for building prototypes and getting innovative solutions into the hand of your users. It is the foundation of execution and will be important to developing possible goals and tactics that give shape to your choices.

4. Prototype: In the prototype mode you build a model of one or more of your ideas to share with others. A prototype can be as simple as an initial design draft or a short-term trial. In schools, I encourage inexpensive "low-stakes" and "localized" small-scale prototypes that are quick to make or trial balloon (think in terms or minutes, a class period or a couple of weeks) but can generate useful reactions and feedback from students, teachers, and parents. Imagine experimenting for one day or one week with a change in your class scheduling to test your ideas. Or find time for a three-week "projects-only" period to explore a project-based learning model. A prototype can be anything that a user can interact with—from a wall of Post-it notes, a role-playing activity, or a storyboard, to a test protocol to better administer a meeting. In later stages, both your prototype and questions will get more refined as you receive feedback from the users. Think of your one-page strategy draft as your first prototype.

5. Test: During the test mode you formally and informally solicit feedback about your prototypes from your users and have another opportunity to build empathy for the people you are designing for. You will continue to ask "Why?" and focus on what you can learn about what works, fails, or has potential. *A rule of thumb: Always prototype as if you know you're right, but test as if you know you're wrong.* Testing is the chance to refine your solutions and make them better.

Your ability to understand your school through design thinking will not only create a vibrant, effective strategic design which inspires and binds your school community, but will also serve as a model of deeper learning. A design thinking approach helps you learn continuously, which is why it's essential to strategic planning. You will learn to correctly identify problems and create strategies to resolve them. For example, your school might be facing problems like underfunding, underenrollment, poor student outcomes, or poor facilities. An effective strategic design process helps you to define and understand your challenges with accuracy: it helps you to understand their root causes, and then evaluate the best of many pathways to tackle them. Moreover, through the process of design thinking you'll learn a lot about who can actually do the work, and you'll be better positioned to match your best people with the best choices.

And There's More

In this book you will also learn how to use your strategy to drive implementation. It's one thing to be strategic and to lay out big beautiful commitments on paper about where you're going, but it's quite another thing to execute successfully. We'll help you to build the capacity you need to be successful.

You will learn how to engage your community—parents, students, faculty, staff, and alumni—to include them in the process. Schools are complex ecosystems, and you must bring your ecosystem along with you in the process of strategic design. You need your *community* to understand why you're doing what you're doing, and work with it to see how your strategic design serves its interests.

Lastly, you will have assessment tools to make sure that you're on track at every step of the process. It's not enough to make a plan, or even execute your plan: you've got to make a plan that seeks outcomes you can measure.

STRATEGY DEFINED

....

Most schools do not make time in the normal course of operations to take a "big picture" view and act strategically. This is fine when everything about your school is working, but as we confront new and unfamiliar challenges, incremental improvement is no longer enough. Strategy is essential, and it's worth taking a moment to make sure everyone involved has a shared understanding of what strategy is.

Strategy demands that you look outside your four walls and make new choices beyond the things you are already doing to be a school. It involves bringing everyone at the school together in an active process to imagine a new future. The process involves deep learning, creation, reflection, implementation, more reflection, and often, revision. Most important, it requires a commitment to the dynamic potential of your school community, a clearly defined filter through which to make—and ultimately implement—difficult decisions and choices that focus your energies. That filter is best understood as the core values or principles that define the organization.

Steve Jobs illustrated the value of a clear strategic filter, which was grounded in his principles. When Apple started working on the iPhone, Jobs shared his vision for a product that would, first and foremost, delight the user. He believed that aesthetics and design were as important as technical excellence. His vision was less about developing a computer that was also a phone, and more about introducing a new product that would both change people's lives *and* be beautiful. Most other phone manufacturers had not concentrated their efforts on these aspects of the user experience. They focused on achieving high levels of technical performance, but they never thought about how the product would make a consumer *feel* while they were using it. Jobs's strategy of prioritizing beautiful design in combination with technical performance was a brand-new choice that has had enormous positive effects on the company and the world.

Why Schools Need Strategy

Education is undergoing enormous change. Competition is on the rise as charter schools, public schools, and private schools compete for students and resources. Across the educational landscape, schools are plagued by a variety of questions related to the twin problems of securing long-term funding and ensuring excellent outcomes, access, and affordability—all within the larger context of questions surrounding the what, why, and how of school. I have yet to encounter a single Principal, Trustee, or Head of School who does not name financial sustainability as a major priority. It doesn't matter what kind of school it is: boarding or day, urban or rural, new schools or century-old schools are all facing this challenge. Schools that have a significant endowment and deep wait lists are just as concerned as schools that are struggling with enrollment and managing worrisome debt.

One way schools attempt to meet the challenges ahead is to attract and serve as many potential audiences as possible by adding programs, constructing facilities, and chasing trends. This "all things to all people" pursuit is noble, but it breeds strategic incoherence and often results in mission creep, where schools pursue activities that may or may not be truly important to their success. Schools might create programs, institute practices and procedures, and designate part-time directors to lead activities only to end up depleting their resources, confusing people about who they are and what they are meant to do, exhausting students and teachers, and complicating the organization.

Although it's desirable to be inclusive of many needs and interests, it doesn't mean you must individualize every offering or compete by offering families and students seemingly unlimited choices. Doing everything in order to compete is a trap, preventing you from making the hard choices that will ultimately help you thrive.

Although some schools reap a degree of pedagogical and financial benefits from increasing their offerings and building new facilities, related educational expenses have risen much faster than the flat inflationary climate. Schools have plunged into capital campaigns to construct, expand, and renovate facilities. The ratio of non-teaching staff to students has grown substantially, from student support (wellness, inclusion initiatives, learning specialists) to external affairs (admissions, advancement, communications) to operations (human resources, facilities, technology). Finally, administrative salaries have increased dramatically: Heads of School were suddenly making six-figure salaries as Boards began to refashion the position as the Chief Executive Officer of a business rather than the Headmaster of a teaching faculty. All of these additional costs have given rise to staggering tuition increases, shrinking pools of full-pay applicants, and slackened financial stability. Clearly, we need to try something new.

Designing strategy requires you to consider an entirely different tactic: differentiation combined with a clear purpose. Roger Martin, Dean of the Rotman School of Management at the University of Toronto, talks about strategy as a means to make very clear choices that define what you will and will not do, thus focusing your energies and resources. He argues that strategic design fosters innovation, or the capacity to achieve new outcomes with new capacities. Nowhere is this more important than in the transformation of the educational experience, where well-executed strategy can heighten student engagement and achievement through improved pedagogy and school culture.

From Sustainability to Thriveability

My model for strategic design shifts the focus from financial sustainability—how we can ensure that the school will survive or operate within a fixed budget—to what I call *thriveability*—how we can ensure that the school is genuinely successful, both now and in the future. To thrive, we have to reconsider long-held assumptions about educational philosophy and organizational strategy. To thrive, schools may need to pause, do serious diagnostics, and even perform some surgery and rehabilitation.

Most schools are overlooking the right questions as they leap to solutions and, as a result, they address the wrong problems. Only after asking the right questions can schools emerge with a strong vision, the capacity to execute a financially rational strategy, and a value proposition that delivers on the student outcomes that matter. The conversation needs to pivot from the standard set of concerns around financial sustainability to a framework that allows us to better identify and tackle the new set of challenges that today's independent schools face. For example, when a school wants to grow its endowment, I let them know that particular desire isn't a strategy, it's an outcome. Then I help them devise a strategy that will allow them to achieve their desired outcome, and show them how to link the strategy to both their talent—the leadership, faculty, and staff—and core commitments of the school. In this way, they are not diluting their efforts with peripheral or irrelevant choices.

LET'S START THE STRATEGY CONVERSATION. INSTEAD OF FIGURING OUT HOW YOUR SCHOOL WILL IMPROVE WHAT IT ALREADY DOES TODAY, THINK ABOUT THESE QUESTIONS:

» **What do you anticipate your students will need for the future?**

» **What's your vision for the next five years that addresses these future needs? What matters most?**

» **What do you value above all as an institution?**

» **What does your institution already do that is innovative, valuable, and distinctive relative to other schools? How do these activities or assets make you successful today?**

» **How do you know your school is strong? How can you explain why your community and culture are your distinguishing assets?**

» **What other questions must you pursue to understand how you might be successful in the future? What assumptions must you test?**

This book is going to help you answer these questions and dozens more, in a unique and novel way. Every day, I help schools reframe their planning tendencies into an active process of designing strategy. I help them distinguish between strategy and results—and I help them change their conversation at every level of the organization, from the boardroom to the classroom.

When I first pose these questions to clients, they reflexively tell us about their wonderful communities, their great teachers, or strong academics. But it is very hard for them to tell us specifically what they do that's different from other schools, or how they know that these things are truly effective. Moreover, when asked what sets their school apart from other schools, they tend to describe general qualities based on feeling or perception. It is difficult for them to be precise about why they do what they do, how this sets their school apart from other schools, or makes a critical difference in the student experience. Ask them why they offer financial aid, or why they segregate students by perceived ability, or why they require service-learning as an extracurricular, and answers will range from "I'm not sure" to "Because we always have." It's at that moment that they realize that they don't have a strategy at all.

Tackling Adaptive Challenges

In his book, *Leadership Without Easy Answers*, Ronald Heifetz, founding director of Harvard's Center for Public Leadership at the John F. Kennedy School of Government, argues that organizations are faced with two types of challenges: technical and adaptive.

Technical challenges are the ones that you've seen before, for which there are clear and ready solutions. Solving technical challenges is what has been at the forefront of the strategic planning process for most schools. One example is a gym in disrepair. The technical solution is to raise some money and build a new gym. Schools also see financial issues as technical challenges that require technical responses. For example, if enrollment is down, a school might rethink its marketing strategy, which in turn leads to solutions such as redesigning its website and hiring additional admissions and communications staff members.

Although schools are great at meeting technical challenges, they are not set up to effectively confront *adaptive challenges*, that is, those that are new and do not have knowable solutions at the outset. In order to meet adaptive challenges, your organization needs to be facile, willing to learn, and ready to innovate. It requires asking new questions, new learning, creativity, and flexible thinking. An adaptive challenge might be "What kind of school will prepare students for a radically different economy?" or "How can we continue to raise tuition in an economy and marketplace where expectations are changing, options are multiplying, and people can no longer afford the price we set?"

Tackling the adaptive challenges that schools currently face is an inherently difficult process. It may require calling into question fundamental ideas about the identity and effectiveness of your school. This self-analysis may then lead to difficult conversations and even some conflict, especially when you challenge long-held assumptions. But the economic and societal drivers at the heart of the financial sustainability crisis demand this level of reflection and assessment, and if you want your school to thrive, you must embrace this process intentionally, thoughtfully, and proactively.

I've identified three interrelated adaptive challenges as the most important opportunities that schools face today: talent, deeper learning, and equity in learning:

1. Talent and strategic talent development are often the most overlooked and underleveraged assets in schools. Without the right people ready to design new and better learning experiences, it will be difficult for your school to thrive. I don't confine the definition of talent to the paid adults; I include students, parents, and other community members as well.

A key part of leveraging human capital involves streamlining a school's organizational design. Complicated organizational design breeds siloed functions, simplistic behaviors, reactivity/passivity, confusion, and a culture of workarounds. A simpler organization, on the other hand, facilitates transparency, clarity of purpose, clear communication, collaboration, and a creative, entrepreneurial spirit. Management is straightforward, leadership is focused, and faculty/staff are highly engaged with a sense of ownership and the freedom to do their best work.

Talent is the key to good strategic design execution. To borrow from leadership theorist Jim Collins and his work *Good to Great* and *Built to Last*, organizational success relies on having the "right people in the right seats" on the bus. Too often, strategy fails because it is designed without active input from the people who will lead you forward through its execution. I don't want you to do any strategic design work without simultaneously asking yourself, "Do we have the capacity to execute?" In this book you will learn what you need to do to design for execution, not just for lofty rhetoric or a business-as-usual task list.

Once you have the right people engaged, the task becomes learning how to harness their talents and combine them in ways that expand and deepen your capacity. How do you unify talent in purpose and stimulate learning, creative conflict, deep collaboration, and action? How do you grow these powerful resources, capitalize on them, and provide all the necessary conditions to foster success? And finally, how do you ensure that your talent culture supports your vision for success?

2. Deeper Learning: Artful pedagogy and design are essential to promote deeper learning skills in students. The William and Flora Hewlett Foundation has broadly defined *deeper learning* as evidence of content mastery, complex problem solving, collaboration, communication, learning how to learn, and the possession of a confident growth mindset. Deeper learning outcomes are essential for students to thrive in the uncertainty of future labor markets and rapid social change. These outcomes rely on educators who can design and implement, and combine and integrate, multiple skills, tools, and techniques, and who can create the right conditions for learning. This is why tackling the adaptive challenge of talent is a crucial piece of the puzzle: without the right people on board—and substantial support for their professional development—implementing effective pedagogy that drives deeper learning will be nearly impossible.

3. Equity in Learning: Schools that want to pursue deeper learning need to open their doors to a wider range of students from diverse backgrounds and experiences, and focus on building healthy communities that afford all students the best conditions for learning. Though this dimension of equity can become politicized, we know that broad diversity in the student body, including gender, race, ethnicity, identity, socioeconomic background, perspectives, and learning preferences, results in more innovation, improved problem

solving and a wide range of other 21ˢᵗ century learning outcomes. Schools that pursue and achieve deeper, equitable learning will seek and train skilled faculty who can facilitate and coach students to solve joint problems in diverse groups, developing vital skills that go well beyond subject matter expertise delivered through traditional instruction.

Tackling these three adaptive challenges will ultimately lead to sustainability and thriveability. By attracting, retaining, and developing talent, schools will be able to focus on what they are good at, and become great at it. And, a visibly fantastic school community with a student-centered program, innovative faculty, and successful learning outcomes will ensure that families continue to choose your school for their children, now and in the future.

Strategy Requires Organizational Learning

To fully thrive, schools need to be relevant and valuable for students and families today and ready to serve the students and families of tomorrow. Without evidence that what your school offers is both valuable over time and responsive to student needs, the key indicators for sustainability—such as endowment growth or admissions demand—are likely to be irrelevant in the near term or unsustainable over time.

I've discovered that what today's students (Gen Z) need to learn now and for the future may not be fully addressed in most schools. Not surprisingly, given the rapid changes in the workplace, what Gen X and Millennial parents want for their children is changing, too. Most look for a healthy, diverse school environment, question the effects of standardized testing, and many are opting out of traditional models altogether. They want their children to be emotionally intelligent, culturally literate, creative, and engaged—and expect challenge that goes well beyond rote memorization, worksheets, and lectures. They are primed to see the value in moving away from traditional, teacher-centered pedagogy and testing as the central form of assessment.

In the face of changing core student outcomes and parental expectations, I believe continuous learning is critical to successful strategic design. My approach to strategic design requires that the school environment becomes a learning environment for everyone—adults and students. Schools that thrive see every member of the community as a learner and foster the best conditions for learning everywhere. In fact, the fastest route to great outcomes is between engaged adults and engaged students who are learning together. Become a school that learns and you will be a far more robust organization, one that is effective, innovative, and creative. The adaptive work for schools is learning what must be preserved and what is needed for the future—and then shifting to how best to do the work. Only then can schools refocus attention, energy, and resources on the factors that matter most.

So what are the characteristics of learning organizations? Surprisingly, they don't look like traditional schools. So before you redesign your school for learning, you first need to embrace a learning identity. Great learners are willing to look outside of schools for ideas, inspiration, and exemplars of practice. And great learners know what's happening in their schools. They are not isolated inside their classrooms or administrative offices. They are constantly asking why. They know how to really listen to what people have to say and are trained to put preconceived assumptions aside.

The strategic design process will help you reimagine the structures and systems that sustain and nurture a great learning culture. Prepare to foster dialogue with all members of your ecosystem so that you are learning together continuously. Prepare to confront the barriers and break them down so you can work in a structure and system where learning is organic and where you are naturally collaborative and generative.

Notes:

CREATE CONDITIONS TO LEARN

When I begin to work with schools, I start by defining the conditions that are going to make the strategic design process most successful. The most important condition is that together we enter the work as learners engaged in a process of exploration, discovery, and creation. Moreover, I start by making sure to establish a shared perspective for the way to define and think about strategy in general, and the way to approach the questions, challenges, and opportunities we will confront.

Strategy is all about the "how." An effective strategy describes the key choices or commitments you make that, in combination, will result in the outcomes you envision for your school and your students. Importantly, it also filters out what you will *not* do. Schools are infamously additive in their approach. I want you to be focused and ruthlessly clear about what matters most to you.

Your strategic design is the overall frame in which you will work—it *describes* where you are going and why. It clarifies where you will focus your energies. It establishes clear boundaries for what you will accomplish. Planning is about actually doing the work: it's a dynamic process to break down strategy into goals and action steps, learning and adapting these as you progress. Think of the strategic design as the frame, and planning as the process by which you paint the picture within the frame.

You'll work hard to identify what you do now, what you need to start doing, and what you need to let go of in order to achieve your vision. And as you bring your school into alignment toward that vision, you'll produce the outcomes that matter most—linking the "why" to the "what" and the "how." A viable and clearly reasoned strategic design makes the hard part of execution a lot easier to tackle.

Demystifying the Language of Strategic Design

Strategic design begins with a new understanding of familiar terms. It helps the community use words in the right context, and then identify the role each person plays in the strategic design process.

VISION: *Strategic design always starts with identifying a vision: what success looks like for you and how you will know that you've achieved it. Therefore, your vision must include a description of success that is measurable and for which you can provide evidence.*

Schools often make the mistake of using their mission statement as their vision. The problem, however, is that a mission statement is often unquantifiable and has a radically different purpose. In strategic design, vision describes what success will be in the future and why that matters. Vision is a way to carry out your mission statement.

For instance, one school told me that its vision and mission were the same: "We will be the school of the twenty-first century whose graduates will lead and solve the complex challenges of the world before us." This statement sounds impressive, but it is rife with problems. First, it is too broad. What are the complex challenges they are preparing graduates for? Whom will they lead? And to be a "school of the twenty-first century" sounds more like marketing than a core purpose. Most important, there is no way to measure being a "school of the twenty-first century." Moreover, the school was not measuring whether or not its graduates were leading and solving problems in the world, so there was no commitment to this statement. This was neither mission nor vision and, while it may make good marketing copy, it doesn't make a strategy. Here's an example of a strong vision statement from one of my client schools, Germantown Academy: "Germantown Academy will distinguish itself as a leader in student engagement." This statement describes success, it can be measured, and it acts as means by which to advance the school's mission and core purpose, which is to "…inspire students to be independent in thought, confident in expression, compassionate in spirit, collaborative in action, and honorable in deed."

MISSION: *A mission is your core purpose. In a school environment, your mission articulates what you exist to do and whom you serve. As you can see from the example above, Germantown Academy's mission addresses both. Together with vision, the mission serves as a guide to all your school's programming.*

Another mission, such as "We are a college preparatory school for students with diagnosed learning disabilities," is as clear as it gets. Sometimes schools create a mission that is more aspirational and harder to demonstrate: "We educate students so that they discover their passions, become lifelong learners, and global leaders of the highest character." When it comes to crafting a mission, you'll learn that simplicity and specificity rule—less is more.

It's likely you already have a mission statement. It may or may not be relevant, clear, or authentic. The strategic design process will help you test your mission, but I encourage you to "back into mission" rather than begin with it. I want you to start with values and vision, because if your core purpose needs to be revisited and clarified, this fact will reveal itself as you move through this process.

Organizational leadership expert Jim Collins, in his 2000 *Forum* article "Aligning Actions and Values," is my guide in the values conversation. He reminds us that values are always "uncovered": "First, you cannot 'set' organizational values, you can only discover them. Nor can you 'install' new core values into people. Core values are not something people 'buy in' to." Because values are embedded in—and embody—how your school actually works and how students, staff, and families feel about their everyday experience, articulating values will force your leadership to reacquaint themselves with their community and try to connect everyone to the planning process in some capacity.

Some schools have stated values. In those situations, I push schools by asking: "Are the values you have articulated right for your school? Let's test them. Let's go into your community. Let's ask if they resonate. Let's see if they show up in the way you operate. Do they really exist? Do we really believe them?"

In many cases, schools often assume they have values, and that their values are apparent in their mission. Yet in some cases, schools have never articulated their core values or described how they show up in practice. Or, the values don't exist in the way they are defined. Every school can improve its self-understanding by reflecting on how "official" values drive the daily work of the school or might be inhibited by contrary "implicit" values or practices.

Collins continues:

> Identifying misalignments means looking around the organization, talking
> to people, getting input, and asking, "If these are our core values and this
> is fundamentally why we exist, what are the obstacles that get in our way?"
> For instance, many organizations say they respect and trust their people
> to do the right thing, but they undermine that statement by doing X, Y,
> and Z. The misalignments exist not because the statements are false: these
> companies believe what they say. The misalignments occur because years
> of ad hoc policies and practices have become institutionalized and have
> obscured or worked in opposition to the firm's underlying values.

The deepest, hardest work of strategic design is in articulating your vision, your mission,
and your values in ways that are authentic to your organization, and clear enough to
show exactly how you can commit resources toward correcting misalignments and
measuring progress toward these requirements. As we move through this process, I
will teach you how to use your vision and values to look for gaps, contradictions, and
connections.

STRATEGIC CHOICES: *The choices of strategic design will be in a
limited number of areas in which you are going to commit resources in order
to fulfill your mission and achieve your vision. Your choices will reflect your
values and will help you let go of irrelevant activities that diminish focus.
Making choices reinforces Roger Martin's reminder that what we choose to do
is as important as what we choose not to do.*

Your strategic choices will drive you to break down your work into short-term goals, tactics, and actions. Goals and tactics should be flexible, because context and available human and financial resources can change. Your strategic design provides the Global Positioning System, but the routes may change due to conditions. Planning is a continuous process within the frame of the design; it is not the design itself. Conditions change, situations change, and you have to keep learning and adapt your plans as you pursue your vision. This is an important piece to understanding strategy: your strategy is not reducible to an iteration of a plan and a list of concrete goals and tactics. Your plan is an approach to fulfilling your mission, vision, and values that will be continuously shaped and modified in response to the environment in which you operate.

These strategic terms came to life for me about eight years ago, when I took my family to Norway, where I was born. I had a *vision* to hike with them to the summit of Preikestolen (the Pulpit Rock), a famous natural attraction that towers close to 2,000 feet over the Lysefjord. The Pulpit Rock offers both an extraordinary hike and a magnificent scenic overlook. I could quantify my vision because I could describe the destination and I knew we would achieve the goal when I got to the top of the Pulpit Rock. I could take a photo of all us at the summit as evidence and show others that we got there.

My *mission* was to create a shared experience that would allow my family to learn a little more about the place I'm from. There was total buy-in from the family for my vision, although when I come to think about it, each person's particular motivation or interest may have been different. My son might have been thinking that this shared experience was to get in shape. My husband likes to take pictures, so his motivation might have been to see the vista and take photographs of it. Nevertheless, their interests aligned, and they understood how they could participate in the mission and the vision I had proposed.

Before we left for the hike, we reviewed our family *values*. Our first value was safety; we weren't going to do anything that put us at risk. Our second value was that we were to stay together and support one another. This was going to be a full-day affair, because to make it up and down the mountain takes about four or five hours. What's more, Norway is a rugged place: there are no guardrails protecting you, no pristine, manicured paths to follow. We all understood that the only way we could achieve the vision and the mission was to use our family values as our guide.

Next, we started to work as a family and made choices as to how we would get to the summit. We could get to the top by taking a helicopter, a jitney, by hiking, or some combination. There were also different routes we could take up the mountain. We decided to hike the whole way, but to follow one of the easier paths, because that was more in alignment with our mission, vision, and values.

When we started our hike, it was a beautiful, sunny day. We set a *goal* to have lunch at a particular spot, but it started to rain, and we were forced to keep moving. Soon the weather completely shifted: it was cold and the ground became slippery (this was when I had my A-ha! moment about the operational meaning of mission, vision, values, and choices). As we hiked, the fog and rain persisted and the visibility decreased. At one point we had to change our tactics entirely in order to move forward; we changed our route and had to slow down so that everyone could stay together. We had to make a lot of decisions as we went up, and frankly, if the weather deteriorated further, we would have abandoned the vision to honor our value of safety. But we stayed committed to the mission, we held on to our values, stayed safe and together, and eventually, we made it. It was foggy at the top, but I knew we were there when my boys crawled on their bellies to the edge of the summit to look down over the fjord.

Adopt a Strategic Mindset

Educators know about "growth mindsets" thanks to Carol Dweck's seminal 2006 work, *Mindset*. Dweck defines growth mindset as "understand[ing] that talents and abilities can be developed through effort, good teaching and persistence." Administrators need a growth mindset to embrace the belief that they can change their schools by learning new ways of doing through practice, reflection, and revision.

Most important, I want you to use your growth mindset and combine it with a *strategic mindset*. A strategic mindset is a way of thinking that is flexible, creative, research-based, and detail-oriented. A strategic mindset searches for patterns and connections. It is a frame of mind that allows you to drive significant changes in your organization as you articulate the purpose and at the same time anticipate the potential implications of these changes. You will be continually examining what is valuable to your school and why, so that you don't overlook opportunities or undermine your efforts. It involves an understanding of where your organization has been and where it can go.

As you execute the steps of the design thinking process, these are the attributes of a strategic mindset that you and your team will develop and use as you design strategy.

Act Like an Anthropologist

Anthropologists do not simply record the human experience, they want to know why humans behave as they do. Anthropologists are hired by corporations, governments, and nonprofit organizations, and even work in disaster areas because of their interpretive and explanatory skills. A strategic mindset requires that you act like an anthropologist so that you can discover how your school functioned in the past, identify the beliefs that drive your organization, and create a vision for how you can shape its future. Your empathy work is the way into a better understanding of your strategic options. As you dig through data and artifacts, your listening and interviewing skills will help you understand what you find and the values that underlie it, with accuracy.

Encourage "What If" Thinking

A strategic mindset can reframe problems as questions, and use those questions to identify opportunities. It is a unique way to address complaints and worries by finding constructive steps forward. I like to tell my clients that questions are more important than problems, and that hopes are more important than fears. Once you embrace the process of turning your problems into questions, you will set yourself up for finding future-focused solutions.

I help clients reframe their problems into "what if" questions. Encouraging a "what if" approach allows school communities to imagine a future that is not constrained by the current conditions of the school, and it's a great way to define the problem and ideate. For example, one of my clients shared this problem during the ethnographic study: "We don't have time to do interdisciplinary learning, even though we know it would help students." I posed the following question in response: "What if we stopped offering Advanced Placement courses and designed assessments differently? What could happen?" With that question in mind, the clients can regain a sense of agency, reminded that they alone control how they use time. They can also begin to focus on what students learn deeply, instead of what courses they are offered. The school may not end up dropping APs, but other opportunities in the process of learning might be uncovered.

One school that did a really good job with posing the right "what if" questions was Pine Point School in Stonington, Connecticut. This independent school wanted to change its focus, because they began to feel the effects of an aging population and the departure of industry. I encouraged leadership to view its emerging enrollment problem as a "what if" opportunity. Through a facilitated dialogue, they answered a series of "what if" questions until they formulated a hypothesis for their mission, vision, and values might be adapted in their new context. With each of their "what if" questions, they allowed themselves to be more expansive in their thinking.

We grounded our discussion in their research. Their empathy work revealed a strong value for the sense of authentic community both within the school and within the larger Stonington region. At first I guided the design team to a smaller framing question: "What does it mean to be a real partner to a changing community?" From there they expanded their worldview to ask: "What if we created our own community partnership?" This was a different way of seeing themselves as part of the community, along with other organizations. Their ultimate "what if" question was: "What if we opened our doors and imagined ourselves as a school for everybody?" Now they were really imagining how to live into their values!

"What if" Questions: The exercise was fun, but it also led them to think completely anew: they decided to test their own assumptions about what it meant to be a school in all the traditional ways. They asked: what if we were a school for everyone at all ages and stages? What might that look like? How would that be great for our young learners? What emerged was a bold new vision for Pine Point as a center for learning for their entire community. The design team realized that in order to grow, thrive, and produce the kind of learning they believed to be most vital, they needed to place new partnerships and connections between all the school and community members at the center of their work. They started with a prototype for a year round learning experience that offered summer programming where adults and young learners could work together—in special classes, outdoor education, and in partnerships that leveraged their coastal resources. Pine Point is already a more vibrant place because of their willingness to embrace a strategic mindset. By asking the right "what if" questions, they liberated themselves to tackle a significant demographic challenge and unlock a future full of possibility

Suspend Judgment

A strategic mindset requires the strategic design team, and all who engage authentically in the process, to suspend judgment as it explores the "what if" questions identified above. Strategic design is predicated on the belief that all new ideas have the potential to be good ideas. In order to actualize this element of the strategic mindset, I use what I call a "diverge and converge" process, so you can fully explore answers to "what if" questions instead of shooting them down before understanding what seeds of possibility may lie within. By "diverging," you create an environment where all stakeholders can build on the initial ideas, take them to a logical conclusion, reshape them, or use elements of them to formulate new ideas. Then you can "converge," or bring these new ideas together, reflect on what you see, look for the patterns, and establish some clear direction. Your values, and the resources you have, will be your filters to see which ideas are worth further investigation so you can narrow down your options and come up with a clear path forward. The strategic mindset always wants to balance divergence with convergence.

I love the diverge and converge process because it allows you to leverage the diversity of thinking, perspective, experience, and talent inside your strategic design process. You can invite the entire school community into the process: students, Trustees, teachers, staff, and parents. Each group of constituents will come to the table with its own unique perspective, yet in the end, you'll create a data set of collective intelligence. You may come up with a new solution that no one individual could necessarily imagine, but the collaborative process fosters the right environment to build it together.

There's an infinite loop in strategic design, where every step of the process leads to moments of divergence and convergence. For example, when I start the strategic design process with a new client, I break people into teams composed of diverse perspectives from different parts of the school community. I invite them to brainstorm their own "what if" questions. I ask everyone to bring their best ideas to the table, and as a group we see if we can build on them. Then, we move to a convergence process in order to look for patterns and connections. We then winnow those down to one or two statements that we all agree are the most powerful or have the most promise for moving forward.

I've worked with a wonderful school that, like many others, was awash in wonderful but too numerous initiatives. School leadership realized that they needed to streamline their new projects so that they would combine to form a coherent strategy, but they were not sure on what basis to make the right decisions. Through the divergent thinking process, I helped them examine, assess, and debate the outcomes they valued most for their students. Eventually, they were able to identify the conditions, activities, and practices that were most closely aligned with these outcomes and the core values of the school.

When we converged, we looked for common patterns in what they identified as most important. We found one connective idea: engagement in learning. The school community communicated that they wanted to be known for creating opportunities that would engage kids, and this became the core of their vision. Then they really got clear about what engagement looks like: "What did it mean? How can we define it?" This specificity enabled them to use that definition as the filter for everything that they would do going forward, so they could reorganize their assets.

Just Do It

The strategic mindset is entrepreneurial and wants to experiment. I encourage clients to try out their new ideas instead of simply ruminating over them. Build a minimum viable product or prototype of what you're imagining. Test it for a day, or a week, and then reflect on what you learned. Tweak when necessary. This way you're constantly practicing implementation and learning from it.

People who run schools have a habit of overthinking, even with the best of intentions. They'll spend a year and a half with a committee studying what their prospective changes might look like, and then will design and implement those changes, only to discover they made mistakes when they're done. Then the entire project is scrapped, and all that hard work comes to nothing. But if you can experiment with your ideas as you are iterating them, you can figure out what will go wrong earlier in the process. Test a new schedule for a week or a month before you implement wholesale change.

At first, your school community may not be ready for the modest disruptions a strategic mindset might bring. Parents, students, and faculty can all be highly sensitive to changes in expectations and routine. You'll need to communicate how the school's commitment to experimentation and iteration serves the overall mission, and how each inconvenience is in the service of improving teaching and learning for everyone.

The "just do it" mindset matters because the biggest mistake schools make is to uncouple strategy from daily execution. Your ability to execute strategy and your capacity to do the work is going to quickly be apparent. And if it's not there, building that capacity is going to be a core element of your strategic design. I've adopted this approach from IDEO, the global design company that led the charge on the design thinking, or human-centered design, movement. CEO David Kelley came up with the phrase, "Fail early, fail often." If you fail early and fail often, you'll give yourselves plenty of opportunity to come up with a successful way to align practice with mission, vision, and values. So just do it!

Ask Why, Then Say Why

It is incredibly easy to jump into strategic planning with a checklist of goals and activities that need to be accomplished. However, when you take the time to think about why you're doing what you think you need to do, you will start identifying what your strategy is going to be, as opposed to simply finding a one-off for increasing the admissions number or recruiting and retaining great faculty.

Asking why is one of the best ways to weed out an underlying problem. You don't want a doctor who would rather treat your symptoms than figure out why you are sick in the first place. If you jump to identify the solutions to your problems, you forget to test your underlying assumptions.

A school that doesn't ask why is likely to have trouble designing strategy. For example, I hear from many private schools that their strategy has to be increasing their endowment. When schools tell us this, I'll begin by asking why they think they need more money. I will ask them why they value a larger endowment. And I will ask them why they think people should contribute to that endowment. When I press a school to explain why they want to increase their endowment, a myriad of answers, many of which are quite different, come to the table. That's when the work of strategic design really begins. As I engage with a deeper discussion of what all those multiple answers mean, together we reach a clearer understanding of what the school really wants. Perhaps they want more financial aid for students so they can build a more diverse student body. Then the school will begin to see that an endowment, or its growth, is not a strategy, but is instead a measurable outcome of a compelling vision and well-executed strategy.

If a school has an idea of what it wants, and it starts to ask why yet can't find a specific reason, it is a signal that it hasn't figured out its underlying issues or what matters most to its constituents. It needs to do a deeper examination of which problem it believes it's trying to solve and how it's going to go about doing that. These are the type of exercises you will explore in "Phase One: Get Ready to Climb."

Saying why means answering your "why" questions in a formal way, that is, taking advantage of the language of strategic design in terms of your vision, mission, and values. This will help you reframe either the assumptions that you had or communicate clearly why your ideas for change matter.

Communicate, Communicate, Communicate

Beyond saying why, a strategic mindset drives you to communicate your thinking and your process, so that it is readily apparent to your stakeholders. You'll naturally find opportunities during the school year to communicate your strategic planning updates. For instance, schools typically use professional development days: beginning-of-year school meetings at the end of August or early September, the return from winter break and spring break, and wrap-up faculty meetings at the end of year. Some schools, depending on their size, also hold weekly or monthly meetings. The key is to look for the opportunities that already exist and use them to model the strategic mindset, tell your stories, and engage others.

You can choose to communicate in different ways, across existing multiple channels. I suggest that you plan formal communications on a consistent and regular basis via email or in person at faculty and/or parent meetings. Then identify all the other opportunities for engaging in transparent, informal dialogues with students, parents, and alumni. You have to create an inclusive environment, which means you must constantly build communication "bridges" between your Board, school, students, parents, and alumni. Everyone needs to feel included and involved, and if you can elicit feedback that is full of emotion and empathy for your audience in the form of anecdotes or stories, you'll go a long way toward meeting that goal. If you, alone or with a small team, begin taking action and making decisions in a vacuum without telling your story, it becomes very hard to get members of the community on board and invested in the process.

Good communication leads to transparency, which is an important facet of the strategic design process. I always recommend being open and honest, even when plans fail. Transparency is critical—up, down, and across the organization. It's as important to the people who are on the front lines implementing the strategy as it is to your Board.

Finally, communication isn't a one-way proposition. You must not only make your thinking and your process clear, but also check in regularly to share what you learn and remain in dialogue with your constituents. And, in order to encourage two-way communication, you need to make sure that there's a safe place for people to share their opinions and be heard. I suggest creating a dedicated email address that people can use to share their thoughts and feelings, suggestions, and comments during the process. Your strategic planning team can check this email regularly, and then use the comments as part of the project's ethnographic study.

What's more, the team needs to acknowledge feedback whenever it is solicited, so that all parties feel included and heard as you move through the process. For example, if you survey constituents, find a way to let them know what you learned, how you are incorporating that information, and how you intend to continue the dialogue. One of the biggest complaints I hear in school communities is that people are asked to offer input, only to hear nothing about the outcomes or implications.

Go Slow to Move Fast

The process of strategic design is as important, and perhaps more important, than any final "product" you create. Remember, you are designing a plan that's meant to change. As you learn, you will adapt. Let the process teach you how to become a learning organization, for only then can you be nimble and innovative.

Stay Flexible

The timeline of planning and the quest for a product (your Board wants a plan!) can sometimes overwhelm the necessarily measured process of learning and discovery. The strategic design process I use is one of the best ways to discover deep challenges within your system, so don't be surprised if you discover you're not ready to do what you thought you wanted to do. Sometimes there may be necessary foundational work to be done before you can take the next big leap. This might include a leadership/talent need, a learning need, or addressing a problem in the school climate or the organizational design. And sometimes there are profound disagreements within the community about what matters most. Let your plan build from where you are now, because if you intend to execute successfully you cannot escape the process. As you create conditions for success, you may discover there's a new path you want to take, or maybe there's a better path you want to take, or there's a path you don't want to take at all. Each of these outcomes is to be expected, just stay flexible and allow your plan to evolve.

The rest of this book will provide everything you need—from beginning to end—to engage your community, to build a strategic mindset, and live the strategic design process. You will refine your vision, determine what strategic choices matter, and experiment with implementation. You will determine which of your existing challenges you need to address. You will prioritize your choices. It's going to be a road of learning, recalibrating, redeploying resources, and making very big commitments— which can take time.

Usually, a formal and fully inclusive strategic design process will take at least an academic year and perhaps two, depending on how much you want to learn, how much you want to engage with your stakeholders, and how much work you ultimately uncover at your school. This includes the discovery phase, the design work, and the implementation. In that time you will create one strategic design, which has one vision and one mission for your entire school. Then you're going to focus on no more than five important choices, each having its own goals, tactics, actions, and initiatives. But the real goal is to let the process take root in your culture. I don't want you to do this episodically, say at the beginning of each planning cycle. I want your school to transform into a learning organization.

Regardless of your past experiences with strategic planning, know that this time it's going to be completely different. Make sure that you've created time and space so people can contribute, design, and implement. Make the process part of your year's professional development focus for all your teachers and staff, not just another activity on top of all the other things they are doing. Engage students by linking the process to learning, asking them to be co-designers in identifying the right questions, performing research, proposing solutions, and offering critique. You will dedicate resources, from every aspect of the school, toward this goal in a way that allows you to do it effectively, without burdening or taxing the organization. What's more, if you can make it a whole-school focus, you'll be less likely to exhaust yourself or a smaller team.

In Phase One you'll get ready to go on the journey of strategic design, mapping your design process to the best of your ability. During this time you're going to learn your landscape. You're going to examine the capacity you have within your current organization, including your talent, assets, and infrastructure—because your strategy is only as good as your ability to execute it. If the leadership capacity and talent to implement strategy do not yet exist within the school, then the earliest piece of the work is creating the right foundation in order to go to the next level. So, you will first discover if your school actually has the talent you need and the culture for learning and growth to sustain it. You'll set yourself up for success by creating the right conditions.

In Phase Two you're going to start exploring: describing what you see, listening, hearing, designing, ideating, testing, and learning. In Chapter 6 you will listen, learn, and begin to better understand what your school needs and wants in order to thrive. In Chapter 7, you're going to get others in on the work so that you can do it collectively and well. You'll start to make some choices and commit to them, in Chapter 8. And in the final chapter, we're going to set you up to sustain your focus, keep executing, keep learning, and be flexible as you learn.

Notes:

PHASE ONE:

GET READY TO CLIMB

SET YOURSELF UP FOR SUCCESS

I talk a lot about creating conditions for success because it's often the most overlooked factor in what drives performance. So, before you start on the journey of strategic design, you'll have to prepare for the climb. This requires an accurate understanding of your school's capacity: what are your assets, what are your constraints, and who can actually do the work? What's more, your team needs to share a thorough understanding of how your school meets the needs and challenges of its environment. By taking stock of what you already have or can do, you can make smart, strategic choices about what you will need to move forward.

When I started my Norwegian hike to Pulpit Rock with my family, the first thing we did was get ready to climb. There were eight of us—four adults, three children, and one dog—together at the base of the mountain. As we looked up to a summit we could not yet see, we began talking about our mission and values, that is, what mattered most for the hike to be successful. We talked about our worries and concerns. We reviewed what was in our backpacks. We looked at the weather forecast and made sure we felt prepared. We made a list of things we wanted to explore on the way up the mountain.

Then we all agreed that staying together and having a joint experience was the most important aspect of the hike. With this shared understanding of what mattered, we started to climb.

Use the Checklists

For nearly a decade, Dr. Atul Gawande has promoted the value of creating and implementing checklists to improve the efficiency of medical practices. According to his seminal 2007 *New Yorker* article on their value in medicine, checklists "helped with memory recall, especially with mundane matters that are easily overlooked in patients undergoing more drastic events. A second effect was to make explicit the minimum, expected steps in complex processes…. Checklists established a higher standard of baseline performance."

I would add a third reason for the importance of checklists: they carry an authority of best practices separate from the authority of the people involved in the process. Everyone involved in a practice can hold each other accountable.

Managing a strategic planning process that includes all constituents and challenges core assumptions requires deep reflection. The work can be emotionally draining and at times exhausting, and mistakes can occur. Checklists for each step of the process provide a safety net, build trust, and democratize planning. Throughout the rest of this book, you'll find appropriate checklists for each step of the planning process.

Checklists often include timetables. In my institutes, I hand out laminated monthly calendars so that participants can break down their action steps with deliverables and responsibilities and can visually map out the school year. You too can plan this way throughout this process, charting all the different information you collect and the actions you identify as necessary.

Build Your Team

Your ascent begins with your team of climbers, your values, and what's in your backpacks. First, let's see who will be going on your strategic design journey. Strategic design is not a one-person job: it takes a team. The first step in the design process is to identify the team and make sure your school has the capacity to do the strategic design work, from problem and opportunity identification to implementation. Every member of the team will have unique skills and responsibilities. They will help organize and drive the process, coordinate scheduling and outreach, communicate progress and setbacks, gather feedback, and keep it all moving forward. Without dedicated, thoughtful, collaborative individuals who are communicating well and working together, the process is a lot harder.

Your team will develop like an onion: there will be just you and perhaps a core group at the outset, and over time you will add additional layers. For example, your inner team that drives the process day to day may be composed of the Head of School and two or three other school leaders and Trustees. The broader strategic planning committee may include representation from all elements of the school community, including students, parents, alumni, faculty, staff members, major donors, and Trustees.

The strategic planning committee must represent the best of your school's collective intelligence: the people who can provide differing opinions and diverse but essential perspectives. Don't create a team of people who think alike. You want to hear from the skeptics and contrarians, the innovators and the traditionalists, the champions and the critics. Most of all, you want to hear from students. Together, these people will be your sounding boards and act as a filtering group throughout the process. You will come back to this team after gathering information to refine and define parameters for the work. Together, you'll diverge and converge, embracing and sifting through your thoughts and perspectives as well as those of the larger community.

Both your core team and the strategic planning committee need a lead facilitator. A facilitator is someone who is trusted, capable, detail-oriented, and able to steward both the process and conversations in ways that ensure integrity, inclusion, and actionable outcomes. This person drives the work, manages the project—the process and the content—and holds others accountable. Choose someone who has school-wide perspective and is genuinely interested in expanding and deepening his or her knowledge base—this can be a great "stretch assignment" for a high-potential faculty member. Choose someone who can create a climate of collaboration and provide the structure and guidance to make the group more effective, without taking a particular position in the discussion. Lastly, you will need to give your lead facilitator significant release time from his or her typical duties because the preparation, management, and follow-up communication for each strategic planning committee meeting and feedback sessions with various constituent groups are time-consuming.

Build Facilitation Power

You'll want your lead facilitator and others working the process to build their skills for guiding conversations. Facilitation is critical for design and execution because whether you are outlining a process, listening to students and faculty, debating an issue, tackling a problem, or designing a prototype, you'll be more successful by engaging multiple perspectives and leading a productive conversation. You'll need facilitation to lead and reflect upon all of the exercises I've outlined throughout this book.

Good facilitators help you explore all the possibilities, permutations, and different viewpoints in a given context. They then help you synthesize this information, find the places where there are connections, commonalities, and/or fundamental differences, resolving them well enough to help you make decisions and take action. A strong facilitator honors all the divergent viewpoints and then helps in their convergence, guiding the group in a way that allows them to take ownership for deciding what to do next. If you don't have strong facilitation along this journey, you risk having circular conversations and losing momentum during the strategic design process.

Who facilitates? You'll need to spot people inside your school community who are interested and willing to help with this important work in order to protect the integrity of the process. Decision makers like the Head of School should use this as an opportunity to participate, listen, and learn rather than facilitate. Strongly opinionated contributors may also not be the best choice, so look for a level headed and dispassionate colleague to help with this work.

KNOWING WHAT A GOOD FACILITATOR DOES WILL HELP YOU IDENTIFY YOUR BEST PEOPLE FOR THE WORK. HERE ARE A COUPLE OF TIPS FOR DECIDING WHO CAN HELP:

» The facilitator is generally able to operate with neutrality inside the discussion, regardless of whether he or she may have an opinion. The facilitator can offer a point of view, ask a question, but doesn't judge the questions or the points of view of others. This is important for building trust in a group. Though the facilitator has authority to insist on norms and process, I often suggest that a facilitator "ask permission" when switching hats and offering advice or an opinion within the conversation.

» Less exciting but no less important, facilitators ensure documentation and follow-up to every discussion. Documentation is critical because it advances process, collects critical data, creates accountability, and satisfies the urgent need for transparency that exists in most schools. Documenting helps to validate and reinforce what people say, and it honors their contributions of time and energy. As you design the "how" of your conversations, you'll find creative ways to ensure documentation and data collection.

Checklist #1: Facilitation Power

☐ Ask questions

☐ Test assumptions

☐ Stay neutral

☐ Keep group focused on goal

☐ Manage the climate

☐ Listen actively

☐ Record ideas accurately

☐ Summarize discussions

☐ Honor participants' time (end on time)

☐ Synthesize ideas concisely

☐ Communicate promptly

At any given point in this work, you might discover that there is no one within your school who has the time or capacity to facilitate successfully an important or difficult dialogue or process. This is typically the point when people go outside and hire a consultant like us. Often, GLP gets the call when schools get stuck, are struggling to work through a challenge, or find themselves arguing around a controversial or divisive issue. In most of my partnerships, I let the client know that the most successful collaborations are those in which I help with diagnostic work and then support the school's internal facilitators for most of the process. I facilitate at key moments, which can include visioning work with the Board or critical synthesizing and decision-making

conversations with the team. Sometimes I offer inspiration and encouragement. Other times I provide structure or advice that increases your confidence and drives commitment. Most important, I play a neutral and objective role in identifying what matters most, framing and reframing issues, and navigating difficult conversations where outcomes really matter. I believe that the combination of work you lead yourself, coupled with an outside perspective at critical points in the process, is the most powerful way to drive strategy and execution.

Articulating Your Values and Finding Alignment

As a team, it's time to understand where you are and create the foundation for planning. Here's your first opportunity to act like an anthropologist. You'll collect data, take a cultural inventory to assess gaps between the formal and informal operations of your school, and begin to articulate your core values. From this foundation, you'll have the information you need to jump into the next phase of strategic design.

1. Prepare for the Study: Collect Data

When I partner with a school, we review data in the effort to familiarize ourselves as quickly as possible with the school's history and culture before studying the community onsite. If you are conducting your own planning process, don't assume there is a shared understanding of how your school functions. In other words, don't treat this initial stage of data collection lightly. Given the typically siloed nature of schools, use this stage of data collection to remedy misunderstandings and reintroduce your strategic leadership teams to key sectors of the school. You can even provide an opportunity for your colleagues to craft and deliver interactive "state of the school" presentations that describe your current reality before beginning the process.

Call for Data Checklist

Our data checklist outlines the information you'll need to collect before you start the strategic design process. It includes documents, information, research, and existing planning-related materials that will help you establish a context for your strategic plan. Any and all data relating to the demographics of your adult population or demographics of your student body are relevant to the process. As you reach out to colleagues to compile this material, document who is providing what and set timetables for delivery on your strategic design master calendar.

Checklist #2: Data Sources

- [ ] Academic Programs and Initiatives: plans and metrics, student course evaluations

- [ ] College Placement Data

- [ ] Admissions: all data related to inquiry, application, acceptance, and enrollment, and existing admissions strategies

- [ ] Diversity Plans, Policies, and Initiatives

- [ ] Previous Strategic Plans

- [ ] Self-Studies: accreditation reports or school self-assessments

- [ ] Development Data: alumni giving, annual fund, endowed/capital gifts, upcoming campaign efforts

- [ ] Financials: historical, current, and projected budgets and balance sheets, tuition and financial aid dynamics, remission policies and other factors related to revenue generation, staffing analyses

- [ ] Organizational Chart: administration and departments

- [ ] Governance Structures/Information

- [ ] Professional Development and Evaluation: for administration, faculty, and staff

- [ ] Technology Plans and Initiatives

- [ ] Marketing and Communications: plans, branding surveys, and strategies

- [ ] History of the School: information related to any mergers and/or other relevant historical documents or background

2. Take a Cultural Inventory

After collecting the key data and creating a provisional common understanding of the state of the school with your leadership team, let's look at your school. Test your initial understanding based on the documents and data against the perspectives of the people, programs, and culture that exist within the school and in the broader community. Remember, you are anthropologists doing an ethnographic study. The goal is to better understand how your organization actually works from the point of view of each of its members.

For example, how are the key documents, recent events in your school's history, and organizational chart interpreted by members? Culture is created at the intersection of formally stated practices, policies, and beliefs and the informal, unstated manners in which various constituencies endorse or at times subvert the formal arrangements. This dynamic between the official and unofficial scripts determines the degree of coherence and alignment across program, practices, and perspectives in your school.

FACTORS THAT INFLUENCE SCHOOL CULTURE:

» Students: What is the composition of the student population? What are students doing and how are they behaving in a variety of contexts? How warmly or coolly do faculty and administration feel toward the student body?

» Talent and Organizational Design: What kinds of teachers and administrators are you attracting? What are the role relationships, and points of clarity and uncertainty in the organization of leadership? What structures drive or inhibit culture?

» Academic Programs: What are your core and signature programs or initiatives?

» Residential Life, Student Life, and Extracurricular Activities: What are your core and signature athletic teams, clubs, community programs, advisory and/or character development programs?

» **Climate:** How does the operation of the school feel? How are teachers behaving? How are parents behaving? How are administrators behaving? How do the various adult constituents describe one another?

» **Understanding of Recent History:** What events in the school's recent past influence decisions made today? How do various constituencies interpret the events and school's response similarly or differently?

EVALUATE THESE ELEMENTS OF CULTURE:

» How is your school culture working or not working to create an organization committed to learning?

» How does the culture feel? What are the different perspectives on how culture feels among constituent groups?

» What are the possibilities for school growth associated within the existing culture? What are the possibilities for school decline? The limitations?

» How do these possibilities align with the school's existing mission, vision, and values?

3. Uncover Values

Understanding your school's values is vital to beginning a successful planning process. The best way to define a school's vision and mission is by first identifying its core values. These are the beliefs that cannot and should not change—they are core to who you are. Uncovering, confirming, and defining your values is important initial work, especially if the values are not clearly stated or defined for your school and therefore widely interpreted. You'll use the process of uncovering and testing values all through the process, but you'll need an initial basic sense of what cannot change to guide the work.

Make sure you don't confuse values with practices. Your values are the core of your brand. If you're really living your values, your brand becomes clear and evident. Lots of schools present their brand as their traditions. However, traditions aren't values—they are practices. For example, a tradition might be a dress code: your school might have a long history of students wearing uniforms. The question is: what value(s) does our dress code manifest or illustrate? Your dress code may be a representation of your history and tradition, your belief in inclusion, or your conception of respect. However, if your admissions team discovers that you aren't attracting new students in part because they don't want to wear a uniform every day, then it may be time to retire the dress code and adopt other practices that uphold your values and are relevant.

Another source of confusion is when values for students—an honor code or a list of behavior standards—is assumed to be a statement of values. Again, codes and standards are practices and policies. They represent deeper values that apply to the entire institution. Asking "the why" of practices and policies leads you to understand the values (or lack thereof!) behind traditions.

Many examples of defining values and aligning them to new practices come from the corporate world. Take the drugstore chain CVS. In a strategic exercise, the organization's leadership agreed that what it valued most, above all, was the health of its customers and employees. Then CVS realized that selling cigarettes was not in alignment with this value. It made a big decision: it eliminated the practice and announced to the public that it would no longer be selling cigarettes. From a revenue perspective, this seemed like a risky choice, but CVS believed it was critical to living in alignment with its core value.

Value alignment drives you to focus your money, your time, and your effort on what matters most. One of the hardest things for schools to do during the strategic design process is to radically modify or eliminate programs or practices. However, look at these deletions as an opportunity to support your values instead of an expression of personal preferences or interests. Once you have distilled your values, and agreed to let go of what's out of sync, then you can begin to think about and deploy resources toward opportunities to change practices, adapt them, or add completely new programs. For example, if one of your school's values is collaboration, then you must examine your practices to see if they are in alignment with that value. Are your teachers spending time together? Are the students offered opportunities to work in groups and learn collaboration skills? Are collaborative skills assessed explicitly? Do you collaborate as a leadership team?

» **How do you know if these values continue to be the right ones for your school?**

» **Do you have a common understanding of the values, even if they are clearly stated?**

» **With whom do the values resonate? With whom do they not resonate?**

As a strategic planning leadership team, you should have unearthed some answers to these questions in your anthropological investigation.

Jim Collins, in "Aligning Actions and Values," urges organizations to think carefully about how effectively their values shape incentives and influence behavior. These outcomes have little to do with how beautifully they are written or marketed to external audiences. He writes:

> There is a big difference between being an organization with a vision statement and becoming a truly visionary organization. The difference lies in creating alignment—alignment to preserve an organization's core values, to reinforce its purpose, and to stimulate continued progress toward its aspirations. When you have superb alignment, a visitor could drop into your organization from another planet and infer the vision without having to read it on paper.

Your strategic planning leadership team should see itself as just such a visitor and discover if the values that truly shape the culture match the official stated values of your school.

Starting From Scratch: Uncovering Unstated Values

For schools that have not articulated their core values, this is the vital point in the process when you must solicit input from your community and uncover those values. Yet I've found that many schools have not defined their core values in a complete or systematic way. If your institutional values are not defined or agreed upon, it well worth your time to do the deep discovery work with your faculty, staff, and students—beyond your team—to generate and define which values are essential to preserve at your school.

ASK YOURSELF:

» **What must you preserve in order to live authentically as an organization?**

» **What is timeless and essential about your school brand that must be honored always?**

Jim Collins offers what he calls the "Mars Exercise" to begin thinking about your values. He asks:

> If you were to re-create your organization on Mars and could only take a handful of people and artifacts, what would you take? Why?

Ask this question of your team and record all of the responses. Identifying real evidence of your values is a tremendously helpful way to begin to describe what you value most in your organization. The Mars Exercise works well as an opening thought experiment to stimulate reflection, particularly when coupled with a more elaborate Core Values Exercise, which follows.

EXERCISE: **CORE VALUES**

This exercise will help you decide if you have identified your school's core values and if they are clearly defined. You'll be able to articulate why they are important and how they are expressed in school practice. Then you'll need to test this understanding with your constituents for agreement. You'll need a facilitator to guide the exercise and help the group stay on track. The goal is to stimulate reflection and identify gaps in your school's operation. After doing this exercise, you may conclude you need to do more to uncover, test, and better articulate values within your community.

Working individually, ask everyone on your team to write down the answers to the following questions:

- What do we value at our school?

- What do we do that reflects and advances our values?

- What are some wild and crazy ideas for supporting the core values—things we haven't thought of or tried?

Give people 3–5 minutes to accomplish this reflection. Don't be too prescriptive in how these questions are answered—allow for a range of interpretations. Some people may value concrete "examples," while others may describe values in the abstract. It all helps advance the work!

Next, ask your team to work individually for 5–10 minutes on the following:

1. List as many of the important values, aspirations, and activities for your school as you can.

2. Now, review and categorize your items:

   a. Place a "1" next to any item that you see as a "Core Value."

   b. Place a "2" next to any item that you see as essential in supporting the Core.

   c. Place a "3" next to any item you see as nonessential.

Take 15 minutes to do the following in small groups:

3. Share your Core Values and essential activities. As a group, construct a visual representation of your consensus "findings," including both Core Values and essential activities that support the Core. Prepare to present your findings, per the parameters below.

4. Present your findings to the larger group (20 minutes).

   a. Every member must participate in the presentation.

   b. You must pick (and present) a "magic name" for your group (remember to have fun!).

   c. Your presentation must last no more than 3 minutes.

If you've got time, you can conclude or follow up this activity by generating big, wild ideas for supporting the core values. This is a fun way to bridge the values articulation/generation meeting with a subsequent meeting when you begin to formulate your concise mission, vision, and values statement, or consider specific goals and tactics that could form the plan.

Lastly, develop a chart aligning the core values that have surfaced and examine them in relationship to your essential activities and your existing, formally-stated values (if you already have them). You will need to draft, share, and redraft internally and externally with key constituents as you continue other parts of the planning process. But in the end, your school will arrive at a fresh, consensual public statement of shared core values and the actions that support them. This is vital framing language for your strategic design efforts, clarifying and celebrating what is so important to your school.

Case Study: The Latin School

Here's an example of how I helped a school unearth and articulate their core values as part of a one-year strategic planning process. It's also an example of how values can be the driving element of a successful strategic design process. When I began working with the Latin School of Chicago, it had a three-paragraph mission statement but no stated values. As a successful 125-year-old school, values existed, and the strong culture we experienced reinforced that belief. But I realized that in order to make important decisions about the school's future, Latin would need to state the institution's values—it could not align resources, people, and practices without that foundation.

In my data collection and cultural inventory, I discovered that though Latin had a well-earned reputation for academic excellence, both internally and across Chicago, the school lacked concise language to capture its educational philosophy. As with many schools I work with, Latin prided itself on offering a plethora of elective classes, clubs, activities, and experiential learning programs to enable individual student choice and faculty autonomy. But sustaining this ever-widening set of offerings also produced frazzled faculty and stressed students. Developing core values could focus the school and its members on what was most essential to its institutional identity.

I worked with the core decision-making team, which included the Strategic Planning Chair (a Trustee), the Head of School, and a faculty representative. Together, we then built a larger strategic planning committee (SPC), the members of which would be our guides, filters, and representatives. We had faculty members, school leadership members, two parents, and several Trustees who came from diverse backgrounds and perspectives. We used that body to reach out even more deeply to the students, parents, and alumni who became our filters, guides, and representatives to make connections to the larger community.

As a large, Junior Kindergarten-12 independent day school with over 1,150 students across three buildings, Latin's SPC would need strong intentions in designing the values articulation process—and the school knew this would be time well spent. The process was also designed to advance the new Head of School's goals to gain early Board buy-in to the direction of the plan, enhance a shared cross-divisional identity, meet the faculty expectation for inclusion in key decision-processes, heighten the alumni leadership's connection to the school, and engage all parents in an affirming, constructive exercise. First, we created a timeline to set reasonable expectations.

» *Throughout the Fall:* Faculty, staff, and Trustees create "word clouds" (a collage of the most prevalent words that arise) based on prompts provided by Greenwich Leadership Partners.

» *September:* Strategic Planning Committee Meeting #1, including Trustees, faculty, staff, and administration, begins brainstorming using Core Values Exercise.

» *October:* Board retreat, including faculty and administrative representation, uses Core Values Exercise.

» *November:* Strategic Planning Committee (Trustees, faculty, staff, administration) produces list of 10 value "candidates."

» *November–January:* Core leadership team of the SPC begins drafting values statement.

» *January:* All faculty session dedicated to review draft in January. Redraft values statement in response to feedback.

» *March:* Spring parent survey responding to candidates for values; SPC leadership redrafts.

» *Spring:* Alumni board focus groups on experiences at Latin and core values.

» *Throughout Spring:* Gain feedback for draft from all 4th- to 12th-grade students during dedicated class and advisory time; SPC leadership drafts response.

» *Late spring:* Final opportunity for faculty feedback to latest iteration of values.

» *May:* Latin School Statement of Values published with its five year Strategic Plan.

Next, we started on the work of uncovering Latin's values. We worked with the approximately twenty or so Trustees, faculty, and staff members of the strategic planning committee. Because the values had never been stated, we went through a long version of the Core Values Exercise to generate possible values and their relationships, listing them, filtering them, ranking them, parsing their meanings, and defining them in practice. Combining that brainstorming with the responses of the Board to the Core Values Exercise, the initial list of values was incredibly long, with lots of related and overlapping words and phrases. Eight different sets of values emerged:

1. Rigor, resilience, empathy, curiosity, integrity

2. Character, mutual respect, critical thinking, innovation, leadership

3. Diversity, service, compassion, intellectually curious, mutual respect

4. Excellence, adaptability, stewardship, character, critical thinking

5. Excellence in education, integrity, compassion, respect

6. Curiosity, engagement, character, resilience, independent thought

7. Integrity, critical thinking, responsible innovation, community

8. Diversity, respect for others, endurance, pursuing excellence, leadership

Next, the strategic planning committee began to categorize and winnow down the choices from this list and roll it out to various constituencies for feedback. GLP then asked everyone to force-rank the values in order of priority and begin to define them in terms of practice. The final version contained three core values: excellence, community, and integrity.

Once Latin named them, we worked together on the deeper work to define those values in practice and identify what was happening or not happening at the school that needed to be addressed in order to tighten alignment. By engaging every constituency in the community, Latin's leadership earned the capital it needed to address areas where "excellence" or "integrity" were not evident in practice. These areas of misalignment became focal points for the strategic plan itself to address.

The Latin School's Final Statement of Values

EXCELLENCE

» Our students develop the skills, knowledge, and desire to solve complex problems through a global, liberal arts curriculum and master teaching.

» Our students identify their passions, learn to advocate for themselves, and become architects of their own education.

» Our school promotes physical and emotional wellness because it is essential to the pursuit of academic excellence and our happiness.

COMMUNITY

» We support and celebrate one another, and take responsibility for our words and actions, because we shape the lives of others in our community.

» We embrace diversity within our school and in Chicago, knowing that it deepens our learning and embraces our empathy.

» We use resources wisely in order to be good environmental stewards.

INTEGRITY

» We are honest, fair, and fulfill the commitments we make, building a culture of respect and mutual trust.

» We give our best effort, take intellectual risks, and learn to persevere.

» We reflect and live with purpose, working toward goals that embody our genuine interests.

The Next Step

You've now begun to build your team and identify a facilitator. You've gathered lots of data, reflected on the existing culture, and have the tools to identify your school's values and define how they are made evident within the institution. Through your discussions of school values, you may have identified important areas where you need to foster deeper understanding or consensus about your school's culture. You may have identified specific areas of the school, practices or programs that are in need of alignment or elimination in order to honor your values. With this foundation you are ready to climb. So now let's begin to talk about where you are going, and how we are going to work together to make the climb and chart your course.

SCHOOL VISITS

One of the best ways to see what's happening beyond your school is to visit schools that are "doing school" differently. Chances are there are interesting, innovative, and successful schools within driving distance that would welcome you. And if you can go farther, the possibilities expand dramatically. Build teams that can take a day to visit other schools and bring back their observations and insights to share with the strategic design team. For lists of schools to visit, consult GLP's website (www.greenwichleadershippartners.com).

Notes:

ASK GREAT QUESTIONS

If I had an hour to solve a problem and my life depended on it, I would use the first 55 minutes determining the proper questions to ask.

—Albert Einstein

In the previous chapter, we dove deep into what you need to know about your school and what your community values. We got ready to hike. Now, we're going to look more closely at where we are going so we can wisely anticipate problems, issues, and opportunities. We'll scan the horizon beyond your school and start to use the data we've gathered to ask the questions that will push us forward, help us envision the future, learn more about what may lie ahead, and map an inclusive process for designing and executing strategy.

We'll get to our destination by asking lots of smart questions:

1. Why are we climbing?

2. Where are we going? What is our destination and why do we want to go there?

3. How do we describe success? What will be evidence of our accomplishment?

4. What's changing in our environment that will affect our climb?

5. How do the people, tools, and information we have assembled help us get there?

6. What potential problems and challenges might we encounter?

7. What new opportunities do we want to explore?

Asking lots of great questions opens up the strategic design process in ways that feel messy but are critical to developing real strategy. And we ask great questions only when we include a diversity of perspectives. Now is the time to engage your team, your Board, and ultimately all members of your school community in a broader discussion of where you are headed and how you are going to move forward.

You'll notice as you read this book that the questions never stop, and this may frustrate those who are eager to jump into action. Don't worry—we will combine action with questions in order to learn. At the beginning, discovering the great questions is the most important part of the work.

Step One below shows you how to stand back and begin to develop your vision. You'll survey and understand the landscape beyond your school and begin to imagine what success means. Step Two helps you to understand your capacity for change: how hard and fast you can hike. You'll explore your hopes and fears for the journey, test assumptions about your mission and purpose, and assess your appetite for risk.

Step One: Survey Your Landscape

You can't do successful strategic design if you don't explore the world beyond your campus. This includes the world your students live in now and the world they will live in after they leave your school. I always suggest that schools begin with a challenging but exciting conversation about the larger context of the changing world. Connecting with the outside world may seem obvious, and often educators assume they are already doing that, but schools are naturally insular environments. Standing back to examine economic, cultural, and workplace trends, and their impact on the lives of students and adults, is a necessary exercise if you want to place learners at the center of the planning process. With this context, you begin the conversation about not just what or how you want to teach, but also what your students want to understand and need to learn in order to thrive.

I've worked with many schools that have limited or no shared understanding of how the world is changing and what that means for learners. As a result, schools are more likely to make decisions or execute new initiatives in a vacuum without a strategic framework that brings coherence to the many activities they pursue. No longer is it enough to talk about improving what we already know how to do. The conversation about the purpose and relevance of school is an essential condition for establishing urgency and commitment to strategic design and for ensuring a sense of ownership for the changes you will entertain in the process.

In the previous chapter I described how reflecting on and articulating your school's values are essential to a firm foundation for the school's planning process. Although I am presenting the values conversation and this context conversation in two separate chapters, they should be happening simultaneously. For example, as you collect and review the data and conduct values exercises, use this feedback in relation to the research on student social and emotional wellness, pedagogy, labor market transformation, and the evolving preferences of your clientele—the families and children of the future.

The changing landscape demands that your values are based on conversations about how your school will respond and command the changing educational context. Consider the following prompts as you initiate this conversation with your strategic planning team and engage your students, faculty, and community members:

» What kind of school is ours, and what kind of school do we want it to be?

» How do we create the conditions for learners of the future to be successful?

» What high-level outcomes will be the most important for our school, our adults, and our students? Why?

» What must we anticipate and understand about our external environment, our students' needs, and education today in order to best position our school for the future?

» What are the implications for leadership and governance?

Every school must also explore its own unique landscape, which includes the community it serves and the particular geographic region in which it operates. I suggest you take the broadest possible scope, incorporating a global or national perspective (the economy, shifting populations, relevant workplace trends) with a more local perspective (changing demographics and needs in the community that affect your decision making).

Understanding the interaction between the micro and macro conditions that characterize your school is crucial in order to position and communicate mission, vision, and values as strongly as possible in your local marketplace.

» Why is your school located where it is?

» What has changed in the neighborhoods around you?

» What institutions have you, or could you, partner with to advance your mission, vision, and values? What are their needs and interests?

» Where do your students, families, and teachers come from? What trends do you see in the intra-community movement? Or inflow and outflow of families?

» Where are people and economic resources moving within your area community?

» Which providers of education are strengthening, weakening, entering, or leaving your marketplace? Why?

REQUIRED READING

Connecting with the outside world is hard work in the day to day life of the educator, but certain topics are vital for understanding both the present and future needs of your students and the challenges facing schools. I encourage all of my clients to stay on top of the rapidly developing research in each of the following areas. Consult my website (www.greenwichleadershippartners. com/tool-kit/what-we-recommend) regularly for cutting-edge resources on:

- The pedagogical movements toward deeper learning as opposed to single discipline focus and content retention

- The urgency of social emotional learning as a foundation for academic success

- The increasing incidence of mental health challenges for today's students

- The increasing demand by employers for resilience, collaboration, and deep concentration in graduates

- The bifurcation of the American labor market into high- and low-skilled positions.

- The impact of artificial intelligence, automation, and machine learning on the job market and needed skills

- Increasing income and wealth inequality

- Increasing demographic diversity and the value of diversity to improve problem-solving skills

- The changing expectations of Millennial parents and their effect on students and schools

Understand the Challenges All Schools Share

Questions and uncertainties confront all climbers, and you'll notice the same is true for schools. As you survey your landscape, you are naturally going to encounter tough questions about the "what and how" of learning. This is the landscape that all schools share, with its existential questions about the purpose of education that will point to outcomes that matter most for students in the future. For example:

» What are the skills that young people need in order to thrive in a world that's changing and becoming more technologically dependent?

» What kind of knowledge do learners need and what dispositions must we cultivate in them so that they "know how to learn"?

» How do we prepare students for citizenship, the workplace, and healthy adult lives when they leave school?

To answer these questions, it helps to first consider the skills and capacities the workplace of the future will require. Statistics from the World Economic Forum in 2015 are eye-opening: they show that two of the key traits that workers will need by 2020—cognitive flexibility and emotional intelligence—were not even included on a similar list made five years prior as a prediction for 2015. The skills students need to thrive now look a lot different from what schools have even in the very recent past focused on developing. They are not guaranteed to correlate with a high GPA or a traditional transcript. Life skills such as emotional intelligence, cognitive flexibility, and creativity are among the most critical skills needed for professional endeavors in fields that will be expanding the most in the near future.

If what students need to know and be able to do is changing, it follows that how they will learn and are taught must also change. There are fundamental disconnects between how we prepare students today using the teacher-led, content-focused traditional educational model and how we might prepare them in a "boundary-breaking" model that resembles the way in which they will operate in the outside world. A well-designed strategy will incorporate the best of both worlds. The question then becomes, how can we leverage the best of traditional practices in school and blend them into a new model that supports students for the future?

As you move through this exploration of the landscape, you'll start to notice how your school's core beliefs, practices, and programming are aligned and/or disconnected from the major trends. As you identify the connections and the relevant questions that emerge from surveying your landscape, you'll begin to see issues to introduce into the strategic design process. You'll develop new questions and "what if" possibilities as your landscape's frame expands. Keep a running list of the questions and issues that surface so you can play with the common threads and themes. This survey is an important part of the early intelligence that will help you identify powerful opportunities that lie ahead as you climb the mountain of strategic design and navigate the rocks, boulders, streams, and pathways.

THINK FORWARD, READ MORE

Tom Peters believes that reading is an essential activity for leaders if they are to stay aware and current, and I couldn't agree more. Peters related this anecdote in a Business.com article:

I have to tell you a story about a neighbor of mine in Massachusetts who would be on anybody's top 10 list of [Warren] Buffett–like people. I was at a dinner with him 18 months ago and, out of nowhere, he said, "You know what the number one problem is with big company CEOs?" I said, "I can think of at least 70 things, but damned if I can narrow it down." And out of his mouth pops, "They don't read enough."

Peters goes on to emphasize that quantity of reading does matter. "I kind of don't buy the four-epiphany-books idea. For me, the whole reading thing is about triangulation." In juxtaposing different authors you'll create insights that are most relevant to your school and context. Whereas Peters describes reading 200 books (!) on technological change and business when he felt he was behind in understanding those trends, it's understandable that no one on your team has the bandwidth for such extensive outside reading during the school year. But each individual on your Board, strategic planning committee, and school as a whole has tremendous capacity to read a bit and collectively triangulate. Distribute portions of stimulating readings on the educational landscape to different members of the committees and constituent groups you engage and encourage them to share and synthesize their insights.

Get on the Balcony

Schools often begin their strategic planning work by forming committees to deal with specific areas: finance, program, athletics, and so on. This approach has its place, but it is limiting, particularly this early in the process. Instead, I want you to look at all of those elements together—gazing at the mountain together, perhaps from multiple base camps, or, as Heifetz suggests, from the "balcony." Rather than audit each functional area, step back and take an expansive look at how all of your school functions, processes, and activities come together (or not). And beyond the question of internal coherence, examine how well or poorly that constellation of beliefs and activities prepares your school to anticipate your students' needs for a rapidly changing present and future. By examining how these elements operate from above by looking out from the "balcony," you have wider perspective on how your school functions within the larger landscape. You can begin to identify opportunities and risks, areas of friction, and areas of leverage. You can also begin to distinguish between the technical problems and the adaptive challenges I described in Chapter 1.

"Getting on the balcony" is a catalyst for strategic design because it generates solid, open-ended questions about the macro outlook (what if ten years from now students don't require a single campus for their school?) and about the micro (what if we combined our outdoor leadership experience with our sophomore humanities identity project?). It helps you test assumptions you may have long left unquestioned. It generates possibilities and challenges (what if we encounter an earthquake and/or a deeper dip in enrollment)? Combine this perspective with your strategic mindset and you are ready to authentically generate strategic design!

Step Two: Build Your Capacity for Change

Strategic design drives action and results, but only through a thoughtful process that holds you to the outcomes you want. You've learned about forming a team, you've gotten ready to facilitate, and you've adopted the right mindset to do the work. Now you are going to chart your course—in other words, start the work of actually examining what needs to change, and why. You are going to identify and understand the choices before you as you evaluate both your existing capacity for strategic success and the obstacles that may be in your way.

Exercises to Chart Your Course

Here are some exercises you can do to help in this first phase of strategic design. You may use these or develop some of your own. All will give you ample opportunity to exercise those facilitation muscles—so make sure you've appointed facilitators for each one.

Don't choose just one. The power in these exercises (and the ones you design) is in the aggregate learning. Decide how and when to use these so that, together, they provoke the best generative work.

EXERCISE: **HOPES AND FEARS**

It helps to get the worries and the aspirations, the big ideas and the big challenges, and any other insights and questions out on the table early. Creating a safe space for people to speak up and voice their hopes and fears will help you navigate within your community with sensitivity and empathy. Equally important, it will flush out tensions, anxieties, and frustrations about the past or current school operation that might preclude people from forward and future thinking. Lastly, these kinds of dialogues will also alert you to perspectives, questions, and insights that merit deeper exploration. This is an inclusive process that helps you gather lots of data quickly. I recommend allotting about 20 minutes for the process—although your wrap-up discussion may last longer!

WHAT YOU'LL NEED:

A facilitator to guide the work, small sticky note pads (multicolor is best), and large Post-it flip chart paper (or any whiteboard-style wall space that can take lots of Post-it notes and dry-erase markers).

HOW IT WORKS:

Assemble people in a space where there is ample wall space for making notes. On the walls, create a paper or whiteboard space for "Hopes" and another for "Fears." Begin by asking the group to individually reflect on their hopes and fears for the strategic design process (or whatever it is you are discussing). As they reflect, ask each person to write down their hopes and fears on sticky notes, one per note, and then post them on corresponding wall murals.

Once the group has completed round one of posting, ask them to "gallery walk" these ideas and respond, comment, and organize the Post-it notes, writing new thoughts directly on the whiteboard wall space. At this point, ask: "What can we do to maximize our hopes and minimize our fears?" Everyone can then document their responses and keep building on one another's work.

When everyone finishes, gather together to talk about what resonates and rises to the top with the group. What do people notice? What feels urgent? What feels important? What themes surface and what strategic questions or potential choices emerged?

EXERCISE: **TESTING ASSUMPTIONS**

This exercise is an entry point into strategic dialogue and an excellent way to open up new possibilities. It helps you begin to build the "ask why, say why" muscle in your strategic mindset by examining the assumptions embedded in the way your school currently operates. I find this exercise particularly powerful in working with Boards and leadership teams to test fundamental ideas about your school, but it can be equally valuable when testing any number of practices with faculty, staff, and students.

WHAT YOU'LL NEED:

A facilitator with a prepared list of questions, index cards, and pens.

HOW IT WORKS:

The optimal way to administer this exercise is to have individuals respond in writing; you can use index cards (or an app like Nearpod) to collect the data. Remind people to work quickly and offer their most immediate answer to the question because you will be moving fast. If they don't have a response, it's okay to leave a question mark. I usually allow about 30 seconds per question. Sample assumptions to test might include the basics, listed below, but you can modify and add questions so that the assumptions reflect your school.

Start with the most obvious, "dumb" questions and collect and record the individual responses from your team. The questions should pertain to your school so you'll need to develop the right list. Here are a few examples to help you build your list:

1. Why are we a coed/single sex school?

2. Why are we a boarding/day school?

3. Why are we a PK 12 school?

4. Why are we committed to diversity?

5. Why do we divide classes by discipline or perceived ability?

6. Why do we track students by perceived ability?

7. Why do we have an endowment?

8. Why do we have financial aid?

9. Why do we offer competitive athletics?

10. Why do we offer program X, Y, or Z?

11. Why do we offer service learning/leadership training?

12. Why do we do X, Y, or Z practice (e.g., dress code, formal sit-down lunches, Saturday classes?)

13. Why do we offer AP (or Honors, or Capstone) courses?

Collect all the responses from each person as soon as you finish the exercise.

WRAP-UP DISCUSSION:

Ask the group what they noticed about the exercise. How would they describe the process? What surprised them? Chances are you'll hear that it was easy for some and difficult for others. You'll learn that there are some practices that many people can't explain, or realize they're being done simply because "it's what we've always done." Moreover, where there are detailed and reasoned answers, they are often strikingly different across multiple respondents in the same school. What does this tell you? All of these insights are instructive. Reflecting on the outcomes of this exercise naturally drives conversation about what might change and why.

As you think about the parameters for change and strategic design, push harder on the values underneath the ideas and suggestions that percolate:

> What are we willing to reconsider?

> What must stay the same?

Knowing these answers will help you begin to see implicit connections (or disconnections) between your practices and your values, as well as to think differently about which practices and ways of operating might limit your school's capacity for change.

NOTES: RECORD WHAT YOU LEARNED

EXERCISE: **SURFACE THE DRIVING QUESTIONS**

Now you are ready to zero in on what is essential based on the responses you've collected to drive your thinking. In this exercise, you will synthesize the earlier work of identifying your values and surveying the landscape by asking: What are the new questions we have now that will propel us forward?

I call this process "Surface the Driving Questions" because more questions will surface when the process is generative with lots of different thinkers brought into the work. These questions will be unique to your situation and school. Though I can't tell you precisely what the questions are, I can offer some structure and guidance for how to frame them.

WHAT YOU'LL NEED:

A facilitator and lots of paper and pens (you may want to use a big flip-chart and Post-its for wall work), or a Google form for documentation.

HOW IT WORKS:

First, how you ask questions is critical and most questions are best when they are open-ended. Open-ended questions start with the words: *What if, why, how can we, where, and when?* For inspiration, consult Warren Berger's *A More Beautiful Question: How to Spark Innovation with Breakthrough Inquiry.*

Depending on the size of the group, you may want to break up into smaller teams. Let everyone know that the objective is to generate questions that might serve the strategy-making process. The most important rule is that no question is wrong, and that all should be acknowledged and perhaps expanded, refined, or clarified as the discussion builds. You'll want to offer examples first.

Sample driving questions might include:

- How will we become a school that acts as a better partner to our community?

- What if we became a school where students don't feel stressed and tired all day long?

- What if we cut tuition in half? Or stopped discounting?

- What if we became a year-round school?

- How can we create more time in the lives of students and teachers for designing learning experiences?

Ask the group to discuss their own questions. Individuals in your group may want to start working alone and then discuss what they each come up with. As group members "diverge," posing and refining questions, ask them to slowly "converge" around the top 3 to 5 questions they think should be on the table for strategic design. As they move through this process, also ask them to hold two other questions in mind:

1. What are the related opportunities and challenges we ought to be asking ourselves about?

2. How do we ask these questions in ways that are most powerful for learning about these opportunities and challenges?

The facilitator will need to remind folks that at this point you are not quite ready to jump to solutions, and closed-ended questions force you there prematurely. For example: "Should we offer Pre-K?" is a closed-ended question. It begs one of two answers: yes or no. Better to reframe this as an open-ended question: "Why do we offer Pre-K? How does Pre-K support our core values? What does Pre-K contribute to our mission and vision of success?" By asking open-ended questions and listening well, you will gather multiple perspectives within the ecosystem of your school. New, better questions are likely to emerge. If we don't do this work, we'll never ever get to the right questions. If we don't get to the right questions, we'll never solve the right problems.

NOTES: RECORD WHAT YOU LEARNED

EXERCISE: **LEVERAGE, BUILD, LET GO!**

This exercise is a critical tool for your leadership team and Board to focus on while building capacity for growth and strategic execution and evaluating the school's collection of assets and resources. This exercise will bring clarity to how your school will be able to act upon your vision. Do you have what you need to achieve your goals? What resources are you underutilizing? What resources are you maximizing or need to further enhance? What resources are being deployed in conflict with your values?

WHAT YOU NEED:

A facilitator, sticky notes, and note pads (or a Google form for documentation).

HOW IT WORKS:

To begin, ask each group member to take three sticky notes and write down one asset he or she would like to see further leveraged, one capacity to further build, and one resource to let go. Invite the members to place their suggestions on a corresponding piece of poster paper labeled *LEVERAGE, BUILD,* or *LET GO.* Next, divide the group into three smaller teams, assigning each person to one of the three topics (*LEVERAGE, BUILD,* or *LET GO*). In each group, members should look at all the individual responses and then sort, condense, categorize, and prioritize. Each team should appoint a recorder to capture the group's shared reasoning and a spokesperson to report to the full group as you exhibit your work.

Leverage: What resources or capacities will your school leverage? What assets, or combination thereof, should you further commit to utilizing? What reflects the best of your school? Do you have a strong brand that could be converted into more application inquiries? Do you have experienced teachers but no opportunities for leadership for them?

Build: Where would you like your school to build capacity? Alternatively, where is your school underresourced or ineffectively utilizing its resources? For example, do you have a dormant alumni network that could have the ability to offer internships to students if activated? Do your facilities lie unused on weekends and summers, missing an opportunity to raise revenue and/or for other community members to see your impressive space? Does your communications department need to better convey your school's dynamic learning experiences to parents and prospective families?

Let Go: Which assets or resources do not require further investment or could be used up over time with no negative impact on programming? Which capacities are no longer essential to the programming that your school is committed to offer? Is maintaining an array of athletic facilities still essential? Which hardware and classroom technology supports a traditional teacher-centered classroom? What are you going to be willing to let go of in order to focus your capacity-building efforts on your priorities?

WRAP-UP DISCUSSION:

As you get ready to share your results, think about what has surfaced in your work. Which questions came up? Where was there consensus in your group? Where wasn't there? Why?

NOTES: RECORD WHAT YOU LEARNED

Case Study: The Williston-Northampton School

Working with a vibrant boarding–day school, I learned through GLP's qualitative research that for many adults and students there were distinct experiences: one for day students and another for boarding students. I discovered that when the day students were able to fully integrate themselves into the experience of the boarding student, they had a far deeper sense of community. Without that, they felt as if they were on the sidelines of the school. The day school students didn't have a place to go during the day to relax, and often felt left out of the evening and weekend activities that shaped residential life at the school.

The school presented strong core values for community and collaboration. It also celebrated each student's individuality, believing this was a signature of the school's culture. The Williston-Northampton School asked: "How could we build community as we promote and support everyone's unique interests and perspectives?" They recognized they needed to bring the day and boarding experiences closer together after testing assumptions such as: "Why are we a day school *and* a boarding school?" In that exercise, they agreed that the boarding experience was valued deeply, and that somehow they needed to ensure that the experience spread to day students. Together, the Board, leadership, and faculty surfaced the following driving questions:

» How can we make the experience for all students more reflective of an exceptional boarding school experience?

» What if every student, whether day or boarding, had equal access to the opportunities and benefits of being a boarding school student?

» What do we need to change or do differently here in order to do that? How might we make that happen?

Ultimately, the school's vision and strategy was deeply focused on the value of the residential experience. The team made some key choices, such as to bring more teachers onto campus to live, and to redesign the student life program around more campus activities that would require both day and boarding students to participate. They reintroduced sit-down meals to promote community. Detailed questioning enabled them to make concrete, specific choices about reforming their practices.

The Next Step: Outline and Plan for Strategic Design

No two strategic design processes are ever the same, and yours is going to be your own. I often joke that strategic design is the Trojan horse for how GLP enters a school. Everyone thinks they're about to go through a typical process to audit their respective areas and come out with a plan. The reality is that if you do this work right, you discover what it is you actually want, what you need to learn, what you'll need to develop. Only then do you embark on a process that is unique to your school.

You may have discovered in the work up to this point that the process leads to where you need to go, though it may actually look different from what you thought you had to work on at the outset. Some schools begin with the notion that they need to build a fairly straightforward plan, only to discover that they actually need to rethink the size or composition of the school, or that they need to first focus on building a stronger school culture, or that they need to address a deeply entrenched faculty morale issue.

The notion of strategy pivots quickly. What is most important is that you discover what really matters to you and that you identify the critical (and perhaps courageous) choices you must make in order to live into those values. By going through this process, you're beginning to give shape to a vision for the future that is grounded in your values, verified by the current state of your organization, and emboldened by the possibilities you've uncovered.

The next phase of this journey really gets exciting. The "trail map" you will create is the document in which you articulate that purpose and collective description of future success in the form of a vision. It will drive the rest of your strategic design. You're going to identify strategic choices and hypothesize goals and tactics that might be instrumental in helping you get to that vision. You'll do this using your values as a filter or, if you're still discovering your values, as a guiding purpose. And, you'll do your best to get it all down on one page!

Notes:

YOUR TRAIL MAP:
THE ONE-PAGE STRATEGY

Vision is not enough. It must be combined with venture. It is not enough to stare up the steps; we must step up the stairs.

—Vaclav Havel

Any successful venture requires a strategy, including my hike to the mountaintop in Norway. However, usually there are multiple routes and methods that might get you to the same destination. How do you decide how you will reach the summit?

We each chart our course in ways that reflect our core beliefs and unique needs and abilities. To extend the metaphor, will you take a helicopter to get there, take the shortest but steepest route that demands rappelling equipment, or will you hike the north trail, which is longer but more scenic, with a gentle rise? Are you going to carry a backpack or take horses with saddlebags? Taking the helicopter is a different strategic choice from hiking the north trail, with or without horses, and making these choices will be influenced by what we believe will get us there fastest, allow us to live our core values, and optimally leverage our capacities and resources. We will make some bets, and we'll take some risks, so we need to think deeply about the trade-offs and articulate them in our plans.

The same considered thinking is required for your school. In order to create change, you need to consider the trade-offs and big bets that will help you get there. The process of strategic design enables that work, and the plan that emerges articulates what you intend to do and why you've made those choices. It will be succinct enough to focus your entire organization and engage people in a way that's accessible and understandable. Lastly, it provides the launching pad for the conversations and the work that you need to do over the course of the strategic design process. In this chapter, you will be customizing the strategic design work around your community and your unique context and needs.

I believe that the best strategy is clear, precise—and described in just one page. Your one-page plan cleanly articulates your guiding principles and then makes a couple of clear and committed choices about where you're going to spend your time and energy. I don't want you, as the strategic design committee, to build an extraordinarily detailed plan with lots of tasks and goals (that's what others will do when they are driving implementation in Chapters 8 and 9). Instead, I want you to articulate a framework that defines success and frames your choices, leaving ample room within to design, learn and adapt. Equally important, use your one-page strategy to communicate a crystal-clear set of intentional, reasoned choices that inspire, guide, and catalyze all members of your community.

You may be thinking: Isn't this our end product? Yes, and it's also one of your first products! The best results come from drafting this document early in the design process and then revisiting and revising often. By going through this process, you're beginning to give shape to a vision for the future of your school that is grounded in your values, verified by the current state of your organization, and emboldened by the possibilities you've uncovered. So I live by my rule of "draft early, draft often."

One reason to limit this document to one page and revise continually is that your strategy should evolve as you move through the process. Don't be afraid to try out ideas and then refine them. Not only is that okay, it's to be expected. If your strategy doesn't change during this process it's a sign that your strategic planning committee isn't listening to a sufficiently wide variety of constituents, or truly valuing the bottom-up perspectives you unearthed during the ethnographic study or subsequent question-generating exercises. You are creating a living, breathing document that will be the most flexible, most compelling, and clearest way to show others where you're headed. At the same time it won't pin you down to a lot of tactical promises that you may or may not want to keep, based on what you learn as you execute. You might end up with a sense of what it is that you most need to work on, which may look different from what you thought you had to work on when you began.

For example, imagine that you discover that in order to create the learning experiences for adults and children that matter most to you, you'll need to radically redesign how the school uses time and space. You know that reallocating time and redesigning space will afford better conditions for collaboration and extended project work, changing how people contribute and operate within the school day. That's a big bet, but you can articulate why you think it's the right course of action. Your one-page strategy won't get into the specifics of how to change your schedule, or how to improve or reimagine your space. Instead, you will write your strategy in a way that allows for flexibility in execution while staying focused on your deepest commitments to learning.

The goal of the one-page strategy is to concisely describe the rationale for changes in practice and programming that your school will choose to test and evaluate in the course of planning and implementation. David Collis and Michael Rukstad's landmark *Harvard Business Review* article, "Can You Say What Your Strategy Is?" (2008), challenged executives to articulate their strategy in 35 words or less. As Collis and Rukstad wrote:

> Leaders of firms are mystified when what they thought was a beautifully crafted strategy is never implemented. They assume that the initiatives described in the voluminous documentation that emerges from an annual budget or a strategic planning process will ensure competitive success.

They fail to appreciate the necessity of having a simple, clear, succinct strategy statement that everyone can internalize and use as a guiding light for making difficult choices.

The failure to create a clear, concise statement of mission, vision, values, and strategy inevitably results in wasted employee effort, frustration, and student/family confusion as schools pursue initiatives without a sense of purpose and coherence. No matter how lovely the cover art or attractive the layout, no one will regularly review in the heat of a school year the long-form planning documents or marketing collateral you produce. Your purpose and strategy must be recorded and internalized by your faculty and staff if you want to gain traction on the ground.

More positively, a simple, but not simplistic, one-pager will empower faculty and staff to be autonomous, confident that they can make the right decisions and be supported by the administration when doing so. It will also help your organization, namely your faculty, staff, and students, to understand what's important and resist the common temptation in independent schools to add, add, add. Collis and Rukstad encourage leadership teams to acknowledge trade-offs when crafting even the concise versions of their strategy. In doing so, you give permission for community members to say "no" to off-mission behavior and initiatives and gain their support by alleviating the anxiety that comes with the incessant need to do more.

You also want to make sure that you can say what your strategy is in a way that is clearly understandable to all members of your community. If they can understand your agenda, it will make it easier to describe to those beyond your immediate organization, including those who will later invest, join, or engage with you. You'll know why you do what you do and can share that in a way that attracts talent and powerful mission-enhancing partnerships. It's a unifying and magnetic call to action.

The GLP Model for Creating a One-Page Strategic Design

Let's begin by outlining the components of your one-page strategy:

Mission: Your core purpose, your "reason for being." Unless you are building a school from scratch, you already have a mission statement. At this point you don't have to decide whether it's the right or the best mission statement for your school. Chances are there's something in that mission that makes sense to you, and that's fine. For many schools, the mission will be too long—a mash-up of mission, values, and educational philosophy. For now, let your mission be what it is. As we move through the process we're going to revisit your mission based on your emerging vision and strategic choices and then decide if it's properly stated. If it isn't, we'll revise it at that point, and chances are, it will be reduced to one or two crisp sentences.

Core Values: The essential values for all members of your organization that are timeless and must be preserved. Although this concept was first introduced in Chapter 3, these values may be refined as you move through your process.

Vision: Your definition of success, why it matters, and how you recognize, measure, or assess when you've attained it. In simple, focused, and precise terms, your vision articulates your ultimate goal and what you'll recognize, when you get there, that makes you successful.

Strategic Choices/Priorities: The key decisions that enable you to achieve your vision. You will limit the list to three to five priorities that *in combination* deliver on the outcomes you believe matter most. Think of priorities as overarching areas of focus rather than as specific goals, actions, or tactics (These will be articulated in a larger and dynamic internal implementation plan described in Chapter 8).

ONE-PAGE STRATEGIC DESIGN DRAFT

1. MISSION:

....

....

....

2. CORE VALUES:

....

....

....

3. VISION:

....

....

....

4. STRATEGIC CHOICES/PRIORITIES:

....

....

....

Start with Vision

Your vision glues the elements of strategy together around a theme or essential idea and outcomes that uphold your core values, delivers on your mission, and distinguishes you from others. For instance, part of your visioning work is understanding what kind of capacity for change you think you have. You may start out by thinking you want to be transformational, and you'll discover that your school is not ready to make huge changes. Instead, you may need to start with incremental work that positions you to have the capacity to be transformational. Alternatively, you may start out thinking all you need to do is get a little bit better at what you already do, and that the visioning process illuminates other opportunities that put you closer to the transformational end of the spectrum.

You will state your vision in a way that is clear enough for your constituents to absorb and understand. It will describe success in a way that is recognizable and quantifiable. If you build a vision that you can't measure, it's essentially useless. Schools can gauge the effectiveness of their vision quantitatively and qualitatively.

For example, your vision might be to become a school that is an active member and partner within the surrounding community, and as you pursue your strategy you might measure that vision by the number of internships, service projects, and alliances you produce. You might also assess the impact of your vision: the number of individuals who come to learn with you, the number of organizations who benefit from the partnership with students and teachers, and the number of projects completed in service of a community problem or need. These measurements will not replace the standard measures of school success, such as enrollment, but the finer grain measures will enable you to evaluate how particular components of your strategy are or are not contributing to the overall vision.

Though enrollment is one of the best overall indicators of success and school health, it is a summative measure impacted by many variables simultaneously. It does not provide feedback in assessing more specific changes in practice and programming. And that one piece of data, when considered in a vacuum, doesn't say anything about *why* you're successful. It is insufficient if you want to collect evidence of your success.

Visioning Exercises for Strategic Design

There are lots of creative and generative ways to envision the future of your school. You will likely develop your own blended versions of these suggestions or new and better ones altogether. The key is to offer multiple ways through which to generate your vision in order to tap into diverse experiences, perspectives, and talents inside your community. These exercises will provoke your own thinking about how you articulate a vision for the future, often by using questions to provoke big thinking. They can be implemented with faculty and staff, your Board, and/or small groups of students, parents, or alumni.

Below are a few ways to ignite early, facilitated conversations about vision which you can conduct with a small or large group of leaders, teachers, students, etc. They will help identify areas for development, hopes, and aspirations for what can be.

EXERCISE: HOW WILL PEOPLE TALK
ABOUT OUR SCHOOL?

The words vision, "brand," and reputation, are related in important ways. Your vision informs the best version of your brand and reputation. I think of brand as the "conversation people have about you," and this exercise goes toward articulating a vision through that lens.

WHAT YOU'LL NEED:

A facilitator and note cards or paper, or some other method of documentation.

The facilitator poses the Essential Question: *Five years from now, what conversations do you want people to be having about your school?*

Your team can diverge by responding in a sticky-note exercise, first posting answers on the wall to the questions below, then having them circle back to converge and synthesize in order to respond to the Essential Question.

Answer the Essential Question by exploring these surface-driving questions:

- What does school feel like?

- What does school look like?

- What are students saying; what is the student experience like?

- What are staff and faculty saying; what does it feel like to work here?

- What has changed?

- What has been preserved?

- What do parents and graduates say?

- What outcomes are indicators of success?

- Why does it matter?

NOTES: RECORD WHAT YOU LEARNED

EXERCISE: **WE'VE MADE THE NEWS!**

This exercise also relates to brand or reputation but asks for a more creative, storytelling approach in cultivating the answer. You'll need time and materials available to encourage real out-of-the-box thinking and creativity. Have fun!

WHAT YOU'LL NEED:

A facilitator, arts and crafts materials, computers, and anything else people choose to use to complete the exercise.

HOW IT WORKS:

The facilitator poses the Essential Question: *Imagine it's 2025, and you are described on your own website, or featured on SXSW.edu, on an industry thought leader's blog, or in a prominent magazine.*

- What does the headline say?

- What are the other elements, including featured articles, sidebars, images, quotes, etc.?

- If it's a magazine or website, which ones are you featured in?

Divide into small groups and create a visual representation of this magazine cover/blog/website promotion and the supporting elements. Exhibit each group's work (either via presentation or gallery walk).

- What is exciting about the other visions?

- What questions do you have?

» What would you like to learn more about?

» Where are the similarities?

» Where are the differences?

» Can you identify major themes that emerged from the descriptions of your school's success? What attributes or characteristics were most meaningful and why?

» What's missing?

NOTES: RECORD WHAT YOU LEARNED

EXERCISE: **DIVERGE AND CONVERGE— A VISIONING BRAINSTORM**

The next two exercises utilize core aspects of the strategic mindset I described in Chapter 2 to build your vision. This exercise creates space for every person to contribute and establish a "building process" that leverages a group's collective intelligence. By going through several steps of scaffolded brainstorming the conversation will lead to an early draft of a vision for your school.

WHAT YOU'LL NEED:

A facilitator, paper, and Post-it notes.

HOW IT WORKS:

The facilitator poses the Essential Question: *What's my personal vision for the school? How can it inform a collective vision?*

Step 1. Work individually to describe your vision for your school in one to three sentences (15 min.). Write it down on sticky notes.

Step 2. Work together in small groups to discuss your vision statements (15 min.). You may want to post your notes on a larger surface so you can organize and combine ideas.

- Identify where you converge.

- Identify where you diverge.

- What can you resolve?

- Which issues or questions remain?

» Is there a new statement that emerged?

Step 3. Discuss how you will know you are successful (10 min.).

» What defines success for your school five years from now, in 2025, and beyond?

» How will we measure school success?

Step 4. Combine groups and share, as a large group, the various stages of your brainstorming.

» What did you learn?

» What key ideas emerged for your vision?

» Which new performance measures and assessment strategies emerged? What is evidence of success?

NOTES: RECORD WHAT YOU LEARNED

EXERCISE: **"WHAT IF" VISIONING**

This is a wonderful exercise for shifting your mindset and creating the conditions for change. You can do it in several breakout groups or in a single, larger group with facilitation.

WHAT YOU'LL NEED:

A facilitator and form for documentation.

HOW IT WORKS:

The facilitator poses the Essential Question: *What bold, radical, and even crazy ideas might shape our future?*

Step 1. To introduce this exercise, the facilitator should first stimulate dialogue and generative thinking with the following discussion prompts:

- What assumptions about how we operate do we need to examine?

- What do we need to learn or understand better as we look forward?

- What choices are before us?

- What choices have we avoided?

- Given our context, how bold can we be? What does that look like, and how might it change us?

Document ideas, responses and leave them posted for reference electronically or on the walls of your room.

Step 2. Divide into small groups (pairs or trios) and generate multiple versions of this sentence: *What if our school...?* Build on each other's ideas. Rule nothing out, have fun, and don't be afraid to be silly.

Step 3. Discuss and put forward a collective "What if" vision.

Step 4. Exhibit each group's "What if" statements and discuss:

- What is exciting? Why?
- What would you like to learn more about?
- Where are there similarities? Differences?
- Can you identify any major themes that emerged from the "What if" statements?
- What attributes or characteristics were most meaningful, and why? What's missing?

NOTES: RECORD WHAT YOU LEARNED

Drafting Tip: Words Matter (A Lot!)

As you create your one-page strategy, focus on the words you choose and how people respond. One of the reasons I recommend to draft early and often is because words matter, especially when you take into consideration how they will be received by different listeners or readers. How language lands on the ears of one person may be quite different from how it lands on the ears of another. I have been surprised by interpretations of language and how terminology can be defined (or misunderstood) in a dynamic and iterative planning process. Surfacing the variety of reactions to specific language and phrasing is an important step to ensure that your plan is unambiguous and easily explained to all of your community members.

Language particularly matters in the context of schools. We are awash in educational jargon and use lots of lofty rhetoric to explain what we do for students. If you don't focus on the right words for your school, you risk using buzzwords or empty, non-specific language that leaves your community feeling skeptical and confused, especially as you begin executing and implementing. Moreover, you risk sounding "generic," sacrificing substance for lofty language.

EXAMINING THE WORDS YOU CHOOSE TAKES YOU DOWN RABBIT HOLES THAT MUST BE EXPLORED IN ORDER TO ACHIEVE A VISION AND A STRATEGY THAT'S GOING TO HAVE TRACTION WITHIN YOUR COMMUNITY. FOR EXAMPLE:

» **Why do we say we're committed to diversity and inclusion?**

» **What does diversity mean?**

» **How does it differ from equity?**

» **Do we really have diversity now?**

» **Which do we aspire to?**

If the value of the one-page strategy is to empower all faculty and staff with clear guidance for their daily decision making, make firm commitments in language and direction during the planning process, not after colleagues invest time and resources in initiatives that are off-message. Your carefully chosen words clarify your intentions, and you may find that in order to use certain words you must define them for your school. Through the process of drafting, testing, and revising, the language becomes clear, precise, and authentically yours. Although there may be times when it feels as if you are wordsmithing to the point of exhaustion, the process forces you to be as clear as possible about what you intend to do and what that will look like in your school.

Lastly, because drafting and redrafting can be an exhausting process, the core strategic planning team, which takes the lead in writing, might be tempted to compromise on language. For example, they may become lax and use multiple terms with different meanings on issues for which significant disagreement exists. If you paper over genuine disagreement, you are licensing off-mission conduct and communication down the road.

Here's an example: social justice education practitioners note that there are very different implications for a school community if it selects a diversity and inclusion (D&I) philosophy in contrast with an equity-based approach. The terms are not interchangeable and signal a different set of priorities. D&I focuses on building the numeric presence of people who identify differently along various axes, engaging all community members in a way that assures belonging, participation, and enhances the students' understanding for all. Equity focuses on ensuring each individual has the quality of experience and unique resources he or she needs to succeed. Both are worthy aims, and can certainly work together, but they also point a school's focus in different directions. Similarly, when describing classroom practice, "student-centered" isn't the same as "inquiry-based," and neither is interchangeable with "progressive."

Case Study: The Berkshire School

The Berkshire School, a beautiful New England boarding school nestled at the base of a Massachusetts mountain, came to us with exciting ideas about what they hoped to achieve in a strategic design process. Pieter Mulder, then the new Head of School, was interested in thinking broadly and deeply about how Berkshire could become an even more transformative place for learners. He hoped to use the process to focus squarely on the student experience: the residential, academic, and extracurricular life at the school. He believed deeply that his faculty and staff had the capacity to reimagine boarding school life. He knew he had a strong and engaged student body, a supportive Board, and an array of resources to tap.

Over the summer, I met with Trustees assigned to strategic planning and worked closely with the administration team to begin strategic thinking and visioning work so they could offer preliminary ideas to their community. The vision and one-page strategy draft started this conversation. But choosing the right words was a big issue for the team. We started with a long list of ideas, which became much more focused and organized, both in the Berkshire vision and how it laid out their strategic choices. We spent a lot of time discussing the meaning of various terms, making sure they framed this challenge as one that was essential to building a common vision. Numerous drafts followed, with contributions from Trustees, faculty, staff, and students. Great care was taken to define values such as *integrity, respect,* and *curiosity* in ways that resonated accurately within the community and could be easily reflected in practices and actions emerging from the strategic design. Messy work, but it paid off in language that made everyone feel comfortable and aligned with a strong vision and plan that felt bold, authentic, and achievable. By the time they adopted their plan, they were deep into the work of execution with shared purpose!

EXERCISE: **CHOOSING WORDS CAREFULLY**

This exercise will help you examine the impact of your current messaging, marketing, or branding for authenticity, cogency, and clarity. Revisit your existing website, handbook, and marketing materials, and create a list of all the statements you've made about what you do as a school. This can include any and all materials about your school: its history, your program and curriculum, policy statements, student life and extracurricular opportunities, and so forth.

At an earlier stage in the planning process, you gathered this data and built a shared sense of where your school is now through defining your values. As you begin to draft the one-page strategy, it's well worth your time to return to the documents you made after you articulated your values, positioned your school relative to trends in the educational landscape, and discovered areas of alignment and misalignment (discussed in Chapters 2–4).

From this list, see if you can answer these questions:

- What is our current vision, mission, and values?

- What is the history of our school?

- What outcomes do we promise for learners?

- What approaches to learning do we put forth? What experiences do we offer?

- What unique or special opportunities do we promote?

When you can see in one place everything that you say you do, and all the words you use to describe your school and your promises to learners, you'll likely discover a few things. One is that you may say you do everything. Ask yourself: "Do we really do all of this exceptionally well?" You might be able to eliminate some of those words in an effort to focus and be really good at what you do, as opposed to trying to do a lot of different things and not necessarily doing them all well. Second, you might say that you produce outcomes that we all know in truth you don't actually achieve. Lastly, you may find that you're using language that not everyone understands. You may say you "personalize" learning or that you promise "academic rigor" or "experiential learning." You may say you value "diversity." Make sure you can provide evidence of these promises and describe them clearly. More important, ask yourself what's most and least important among your current promises to the community. Can you do everything you say? And how do your existing commitments relate to new ideas that emerged in the early stages of the planning process?

In the end, your website, your handbooks, and your admissions materials will benefit from the clarity, specificity, and coherence that emerges. And you'll do much better strategy work!

Connecting Vision to Strategic Choices

I define strategic choices (or priorities) as the key decisions that, in combination, will enable you to achieve your vision. I recommend limiting your priorities to no more than five (fewer is better!) for the sake of clarity and focus. With every choice, you are also deciding what *not* to do, and it's important to articulate that clearly. Imagine if you—and all the members of your school community—could articulate your strategy with ease and confidence. Imagine how that would transform your community and communication with prospective families.

One way to begin this stage is to practice saying your strategy using the following prompt: *Our vision is ABC because we believe XYZ, and we have made these (3 to 5) key choices in order to realize our vision.*

Strategic choices direct the "how" and define the road map that takes you toward your vision—without being overly prescriptive. Most important, because of your investment in articulating your values, you'll make strategic choices that align. Your choices will uphold and express who you are and what you believe. They will also focus you on the practices and structures you need to reinforce or build in order to execute effectively.

For example, if your vision states that you will design your school on a foundation of student-driven learning experiences, a strategic priority might be to redesign the curriculum to emphasize deep, long term, student-led projects. By definition, you may need to let go of the practice of the single-discipline curriculum and the structure of the subject matter-by-subject matter class schedule. You may also need to rethink how teachers learn, plan, and collaborate to prepare for project work.

Another strategic choice might be to redesign all co-curricular programming, including athletics, in service of your core values. For example, if collaboration and inclusion are core values, you may need to look at how athletics foster meaningful participation among all students and reconsider how playing time, competition, and coaching fit with those values. Your strategic choices and your values are the filter through which you redefine, eliminate, or better integrate activities in order to align them with your values.

I work with many schools that choose to deeply recalibrate how learning happens and unleash the talents of their teachers on this vision. One choice might be to reimagine your adult culture and pedagogical approach in order to attract, develop, and retain teachers/facilitators who can support learning across multiple disciplines. You may decide that to achieve your vision, the pedagogical tool kits and mindsets of your educators must continually evolve, and this requires numerous shifts in how adults choose to engage, learn, and work at your school. This choice focuses squarely on adult talent and mindset: it may require you to let go of unwilling faculty and schedules that hinder collaboration among adults, and professional learning or evaluation policies that don't serve your choice.

Once you've agreed on which choices matter, you'll need to decide how to make them happen. Tactics and initiatives evolve from these decisions, but take some practice in formulating. As with each step of the strategic planning process thus far, they will develop iteratively and incrementally. Execution and implementation will happen in real time as you design, pilot, assess, and recalibrate around those tactics and initiatives.

What About Outcomes?

You may be wondering where you are going with all this divergent work and visioning. You might ask: don't we already know what we need to accomplish for students?

It is good to design backwards from the outcomes you value most for students. Many schools have a "Portrait of a Graduate" or similar statement of what they intend to develop in students. However, I often find these portraits to be rhetoric—form over substance. Student outcomes are usually not the same as these portraits, because student outcomes need to be quantifiable or in some way evident. For example, you may say your learners are collaborators or compassionate citizens. What evidence do you have for these outcomes? How does the learning experience for students clearly deliver on these criteria?

Use this process to continually test, affirm, and refine your understanding of your school's educational philosophy and the outcomes it values most for learners. The answers and the questions you receive from your community as you move through the process will help you redefine the learning outcomes you believe matter most—and then how you must design for these outcomes. With the right definition, you should be able to test their current experience and ask if the student experience is driving toward those outcomes, or if it is driving toward something else.

If this is work you need to do, consider conducting interviews with your constituents to explore outcomes (Chapter 6 shows how to conduct these conversations). Then you can use those outcomes as a guide for your vision and choices.

IDENTIFY YOUR DESIRED STUDENT OUTCOMES BY ASKING TRUSTEES, PARENTS, STUDENTS, ALUMNI, AND TEACHERS THE FOLLOWING QUESTIONS:

» **What do we want students to know?**

» **What must they be able to do?**

» **What mindsets and dispositions matter most?**

» **What is the current experience for students?**

» **What would you like the experience to be and what are the gaps?**

By asking these questions, you might discover that the outcomes that matter most to students and parents are very different from the outcomes that matter to alumni. For instance, your alumni donors might still think that every graduate must know calculus, even though many of your students now lean towards other maths such as probability and statistics. How will you address these tensions and resolve them? Where will you take a stand? Your vision and values will guide you here, but knowing how to explain your choices and to whom is critical to a successful process.

If your school is unsure about desired outcomes or philosophy, this is the time to take a step back. Many schools may have a general sense of what they believe, or where they think the school should be going, or how to adjust to the future, but leap to solutions that may not address the true interests of learners. By doing this work first, all of your other decisions will fall into place.

EXERCISE: **STRATEGIC CHOICES**

I suggest facilitating conversations among Trustees and school leaders in small groups to identify a range of key choices to achieve your vision. It's important to be both creative and inclusive in designing these conversations to ensure broad participation and interaction across functional roles and departments. Ask your groups to flesh out their one-page strategy drafts and present them to one another. Then collectively synthesize the best ideas to emerge.

Ask the following questions to guide your strategic choices:

- What driving questions have risen to the top?

- What do we value at the core?

- What resources/capabilities can we leverage?

- What choices are before us?

- What trade-offs do these choices present?

- What is non-negotiable?

- What subjects of disagreement can be reframed or redefined to build consensus?

- What do we need to test or learn in order to be confident?

So Where's the Implementation Plan?

At this point in the process, your team will be eager to start implementing your plan. It's natural to ask, "What are we actually going to do? I want to get to work!" If you've built a solid, diverse team, it will include concrete-, linear-, and action-oriented thinkers, and they're asking good questions. You need to keep them engaged, but you also need to remind them that you are "going slow to move fast" as you explore the specifics of how to execute the plan. Embrace the process of determining how to filter your tactical options as you imagine the implications of each choice. Don't get discouraged because you are not necessarily committing quite yet. In fact, I suggest one norm to help this conversation: if you spot a problem with multiple plausible responses, name it, and then offer a first step for addressing the issue in several ways. Don't say no to a tactical response outright, unless there is a clear conflict with core values.

This is where you become even more clearly aware of how your strategic choices will succeed or fail. Why? By moving "from the balcony and onto the dance floor" and exploring the specifics of implementation, you can refine your choices and sharpen your vision.

For example, you can begin to articulate and test action steps within your draft (and we'll do lots of this in Chapter 6). Note the action steps underneath your priorities. Discuss order, timing, and method. Test them with your students, faculty, and staff, as appropriate. How realistic are the steps? What capacities or new learning do they require? What are the resources you'll need to do this work? How are the action steps distributed across time and personnel? Learn what works, what you need, and what challenges or bottlenecks may arise. But focus first and foremost on using this information to identify or refine the best strategic choices.

Allow yourself the luxury of time to build the detail that accompanies the one-page draft in order to confirm or refine your vision and choices and maintain the "draft" status. Remember, this is a dynamic, ongoing process informed by continuous feedback and learning. An implementation plan will emerge from your one-page strategy, and it will be highly dynamic.

In the next few chapters, I will move into design, and you will begin to test the options for creating and executing for change. Get ready to open up the process further, and invite faculty, staff, students, and your other stakeholders into the dialogue. As you test, you continuously hold your values and desired outcomes up to this one-page strategy draft. You'll revise, refine, and polish the draft, communicating with parents, students, faculty, and staff as you go. By the time your strategy is clear, you'll already be into implementation and your community will be engaged and supportive—exactly as you would want!

Notes:

PHASE TWO:

GET MOVING

COMMUNICATE, EMPATHIZE, AND LEARN

The single biggest problem in communication is the illusion it has taken place

—George Bernard Shaw

By now you should have a big-picture perspective of what you want your strategic design to accomplish. But to pursue this vision successfully, you'll need to learn more. It's time to do a more detailed exploration of the mountain as you climb. In this chapter, you'll learn how to share your initial ideas with your community, which were outlined on your one-page strategy. You'll ask others beyond the strategic planning committee to test, explore, refine, and expand your thinking. In other words, you'll continue to study your school culture by testing ideas and possibilities to see how its members respond. You are now widening the circle and expanding the dialogue. One tool GLP encourages schools to utilize is *design thinking* while engaging with a strategic mindset, which allows you to both test and problem-solve as you move through this process.

At this stage of the design process you should be ready to test-drive your draft of the one-page strategy in your focus groups. Through *empathetic interviewing*, you will once again retrace your steps in a journey from the balcony to the dance floor, as it were, and back again. Your draft represents your best understanding of your school and its future from your position in the balcony—where you can see all the interactions of your key players and how you fit relative to your competitors. But now you are looking to assess the validity of your initial articulation of constituents' experiences and hopes, your self-assessment relative to external trends and competitors, and your ordering of priorities.

» **How does the first draft of mission, vision, and strategic choices and priorities resonate?**

» **How does it describe what is essential about our school?**

» **How does it stretch our school in ways that capture our community's ambition?**

» **How does it position us in relation to the local market and broader educational and demographic trends?**

» **How does it make us distinctive?**

If you are truly open to the results as you test elements of your one-page strategy, you will naturally move in the empathy mode: the first phase of the design thinking process. Testing your plan as it evolves is one of the best ways to learn *and* to engage your community. It provides a filtering process, giving your stakeholders a voice and a window into the process, and enables your decision-making team to incorporate feedback effectively. I like to test early drafts (or particular ideas/content) and then report back to the community on how we incorporated what we learned and how we're continuing to add detail and design.

The five elements of design thinking—empathize, define, ideate, prototype, test—are simply good practice. The empathy mode should always be in effect as you move through the design and execution of strategy. The point is to use these methodologies as you flesh out your plan; describe your choices with action steps and goals; and build new structures, practices, services, and programs. Let's begin with using the empathy mode and then outline multiple ways in which you can use this process to sharpen your strategy and your implementation plans.

Like any methodology, design thinking succeeds when conditions are right. The following is a checklist of tips for success to share with your facilitators, student and teacher designers, and team leaders when you begin to expand the work in your community.

Checklist #3: Design Thinking Tips

☐ Encourage a diversity of perspectives. Solicit various areas of expertise, different contexts, or ways of working in order to push your design to be more creative and applicable to multiple parties.

☐ Create a safe space for ideas. It is critical for this work to feel generative. Encourage wild ideas and divergent thinking to push the boundaries. In order to promote divergence, impose or release constraints on your thinking to unsettle assumptions (What if we had no budget for student life? What programming would we create instead? What if we had an unlimited budget for outreach to new feeder schools? How would we engage them?). Use the techniques for the facilitation process in Chapter 3, and for asking great questions in Chapter 4, to stimulate dialogue and creative thinking.

☐ Help everyone understand the process first so they know where they are headed and why.

☐ Make sure to consider all your stakeholders. Whom do you want to engage in this process? Whom do you need to talk to and learn from?

Empathy Begins with Good Communication

Empathy work and the tools I describe here allow you to see your school through the eyes of individuals and groups that may very well have a different point of view than you. Prepare to be surprised—what you think is valuable may not be so important to somebody else. Alternatively, what you haven't thought about may be highly relevant or valuable to somebody else. You won't know what you are missing unless you spend time in the empathy mode, seeking input with a thoughtfully planned approach.

As you move outside of the committee to more broadly engage your constituents, you'll need to explain to newcomers the process thus far and the thinking that has surfaced, using care to listen to their reactions and suggestions. Remember, you have been on the journey and you need to wait now as others catch up and pitch in to the process. And, as you trial-balloon specific strategic choices, expect the tenor of feedback you receive to have a different intensity. The feedback you received earlier as you were formulating values will likely have been more reflective or philosophical in nature. Now you are moving in to the details of practices—and that's where execution happens. As you test strategic choices that impact the daily practice and prospects of individual faculty and staff members, their defensiveness may increase and feedback may have more bite. But these are precisely the reactions you need to hear before you commit to choices that will require lots of political capital and resources. Beginning to understand the relative intensity of support or opposition to choices will help you set priorities in the implementation stage.

The time you take to communicate and engage others will pay off in the long run. So take a deep breath and prepare to listen. But first, let them know exactly what you are doing, and why and how you hope to include them. The best way to do this is to be completely transparent with your intentions.

The Four Conditions of Transparency

Crafting your one-page strategy was your last point of convergence and likely occurred within a smaller leadership group. Phase Two is the next round of the "diverge and converge" process and it takes you out into your community. Ideally, it's the point where your process becomes visible to everyone. You'll do the deep work to revise your one-page strategy, clarifying language and choices, and filling in the details. You will begin by diverging once again, this time by engaging your larger community of students, faculty, staff, and perhaps parents and alumni. Before you open up your process and bring your community into the work, everyone needs a solid understanding of the goals for the process. Specifically, you are trying to test an emerging vision with your community, learn more about the needs and interests of your constituents, and surface the choices that will refine your strategy.

I suggest drafting communications ahead of every survey, interview, focus group, or exercise to explain your purpose and manage the expectations of your participants. I also guide clients to always communicate what their constituents can expect to learn or hear following the work. Nothing is worse than contributing time to a survey or focus group only to hear nothing about the outcome of those efforts.

As you administer surveys, lead interviews and focus groups, or facilitate drawing sessions, it's important to communicate transparently. I suggest establishing four expectations in every instance:

1. Commit to Inclusivity: It is essential that when you say you will include everyone in strategic design, you mean everyone. Design your outreach so that the process will offer all of your stakeholders an opportunity to participate. And don't forget essential staff members from your dining hall, administrative offices, or grounds. Include even your youngest students through focus grouping or surveys in which they can draw or select emojis in their responses.

You will be communicating with students, parents, and alumni in numerous ways. I believe in regular and frequent communication to the broader community during the strategic design process. For instance, I often suggest that schools create an information page on their website where they can provide brief updates and people can contribute ideas and suggestions to the strategic design process.

2. Clarify Decision Making: Everyone needs to know how this process will translate to action. In order for the Board to set vision and values, there has to be a cycle or feedback loop between governance and the community. Decisions about how the vision will be achieved and how to execute it will reside within the school. I suggest that you be clear about the decision-making process during these conversations. Certain decisions are going to be made by the Board with the Head of School and his or her team, regardless of the input you've received from outside. There are also going to be certain decisions that will rest with faculty or students. You will determine which decisions are for which constituents, and you'll ground this decision in your core values.

3. Be a Learner: Be clear that as a school, learning is not just for kids! Strategic design, and the work of a school, is a continuous learning experience for the entire institution. Your design process is an opportunity for the team to ask the essential questions about the future, explore the answers deeply, and problem-solve within that context. It's a process for the Board to learn about how values are embedded in the culture and what it will take to achieve a bold vision for the future. Everyone is learning all the time; and it is a condition that you want to happily embrace throughout the work.

4. Focus on Student Needs: Be clear in both words and actions that you are putting the needs and interests of your students at the center of every conversation. Whatever your stated values are, whatever you believe your mission to be, and whatever vision is emerging in this work, you are going to continually ask: "How do these changes serve or create a meaningful experience for students?" Strategically focusing on serving students is almost always more likely to build common ground among your school's various constituencies.

Test Your Vision

Let's begin by testing your emerging vision, outlined in the one-page strategy, with key groups in your school community: students, faculty and staff, and parents/alumni. Treat your draft vision as a premise attempting to capture the spirit of your community.

» How well does the language of the vision resonate? With which groups and why?

» How do key constituencies report that your strategic choices will impact them?

» What concerns arise? Where is there confusion or resistance?

» What excites people? Where is there confidence and support?

Not only do you want to test reactions, you also want to solicit input and involvement. Your initial ideas may not be the best, and as you get closer to the people who will implement or experience your strategy (students and teachers) and the people who invest their time and resources (parents and alumni), you'll be able to clarify your intentions and come up with a better strategy.

EMPATHY INTERVIEWS PRE-WORK

Here's an easy and valuable way to practice and utilize empathy interviews. Have each member of your strategic planning team hone their skills by conducting two to three empathy interviews with teachers and/or staff about how they want to engage in the strategic design process and what their hopes are for the future of the school. Each interview should take no more than 20 minutes. Once everyone completes their interviews, come together to reflect, discuss themes and insights, and determine next steps that respond to what you've learned.

Sample empathy interview conversation starter:
We want to learn more about your interests in strategic design and hope to create opportunities to partner more actively with you. You have a unique role/position here at school. We would also like to learn more about your perspective, interests, and aspirations for the school.

Sample questions:

- What do you know about our strategic planning process?

- What would you like to know?

- How would you like to participate?

- What excites you most about this process?

- What are you worried about?

- If one thing could change at our school, what would you like it to be? Why?

- What is the one thing that we must preserve? Why?

Tools for Listening: Surveys, Focus Groups, and Interviews

Whether you want to learn more about student outcomes, or you want to test your emerging vision and choices, empathy work is your opportunity to listen closely and better understand the experiences and interests of your community. Like most of what I describe in this book, empathy work is ongoing. You may, for example, conduct annual surveys with students, staff, and families. You may also regularly convene people to hear feedback or understand their experiences relative to what's happening at school. These "listening practices" help schools become better at listening, learning, and collecting feedback. I encourage you to be intentional about empathy work as a regular practice to build strategic muscle during and beyond the planning process. Institutionalizing opportunities for system-wide feedback are essential for successful plan implementation and preserving the camaraderie needed to push for school improvement. There are lots of ways to operate in the empathy mode, and lots of tools and forums for learning more about your stakeholders:

Surveys: Surveys are an easy, large-scale way to test something specific, to quantify qualitative feedback, and to generate data year after year so you can assess progress and change. Strategic design is a perfect opportunity to employ surveys. I encourage schools to design surveys that help them test values alignment, vision, and experience, as well as solicit feedback on aspirations and interests. It's a good practice to establish one or two baseline surveys that you can administer annually. In designing the baseline survey, consult with faculty, staff, and students to co-create questions and the conditions for administering the survey so they accept the legitimacy of the tool and participate when it's time to deliver and act on the results.

Conversations and Interviews: You can empathize by having both formal and informal conversations. These can be structured, one-on-one interviews where you follow a script, or open-ended conversations that allow you to understand different stakeholders' perspectives. You can also empathize informally or "in the moment," such as a chance meeting in a parking lot, or the hallway, or wandering around the dining hall talking to students.

Focus Groups: Another way to do empathy work is to assemble focus groups. Focus groups can be scripted or relaxed, but typically have set goals to achieve. You will want to probe deeply with questions, hear viewpoints, and listen to how individuals engage with one another. Focus groups offer the opportunity to hear dialogue—not only where people converge but also where they diverge, and what might be underneath those differences of opinions. In order for your focus group members to be as open as possible, think carefully about group composition and how notes documenting the conversation are handled. As you compose focus groups, show drafts of the rosters with community members who know the social dynamics of the constituency you are studying.

Fishbowl Dialogues: Sometimes the best way to hear from others is to listen to them having conversations and offering honest reflections. This type of fishbowl dialogue is particularly effective with students. Organizing a facilitated dialogue with students that adults can observe is a high-impact way for parents, educators, and others to hear and understand the concerns, experiences, needs, and interests of the people who matter most in schools. The key is to facilitate the dialogue in a way that fosters trust and makes it easy for students to engage with one another as they lose awareness of the audience. How often have you driven a carpool only to discover that the kids are speaking to one another as if you are not there? A well designed fishbowl with students can yield the same results. I have found that students who understand the purpose readily embrace the chance to speak honestly and offer specific examples. Guided by a trusted facilitator, observers are granted a window into a dialogue to which they would normally not have access.

Observations: Another way to do empathy work is through observation. You can empathize in the form of a learning walk through your school, stopping into classrooms, watching students in their different environments on the sports fields, in the cafeteria, or in the art center. Your observations might track how students and faculty interact with one another, or how they engage with learning in and out of the classroom. You might follow observation with additional inquiry through a survey or focus group, framing questions to students and adults about what you see and deepening your understanding of behaviors and practices. You'll be collecting important information about your emerging vision and choices by understanding the current experience of others.

Drawing Exercises: Drawing exercises are a powerful means for surfacing how people experience or hope to experience school by using visual images. These exercises can be especially helpful with young children, though I've seen them utilized with tremendous impact among adults as well. Drawings can be "coded" like surveys or focus groups for common elements. They can have a powerful, even emotional, impact on data-hungry Trustees and faculty who respond well to visual information. The visuals you generate from this stage of the design process can also enliven your communication materials documenting the planning process for the community.

Implementing Surveys, Interviews and Focus Groups

I have found that short, quick surveys and focus group-style meetings are the most effective ways of soliciting feedback for empathy work. With each method, the key is to be exceedingly clear about wanting feedback and why it matters. Surveys give you broad access and a wider response rate; focus groups allow you to probe and explore—and can surface insights and motivations that surveys overlook.

I often combine surveys and focus groups. A survey can create baseline data and offer insight to what needs deeper exploration. Focus groups can then follow to: 1) share survey feedback; and 2) explore more deeply the questions and issues the survey uncovers.

How you ask for input is important. Frame your request in the larger context of your strategic planning process and be sure to define the terminology you are using. For example, if you are asking for feedback on vision, mission, and values, define those terms. If you are asking about school programs, it may also help to define educational language: personalization, differentiation, pedagogy, curriculum, equity, inclusion, etc. In every case, the idea is to ensure that people understand how you are using these terms and what they mean to strategy and your school.

Core Values: A survey to test the values you articulate and how you define them is always illuminating. I like a survey that defines the term "core value," tests the respondent's level of agreement about the core values you suggest and define, and also asks the degree to which the school's practices/programs align with those values. For example, you might ask about a core value and the extent to which your respondents believe that value (as defined) is authentic to the community and manifest in the culture and operation of the school. Surveys can collect aggregate data on agreement and alignment; focus groups can be used to follow up and probe deeply to learn more about potential gaps. Be sure to test values with students. They know best if a school is in alignment.

Outcomes: Exploring outcomes for students and for the life of the school is another means to test mission, vision, and practice. What learning outcomes matter most? What other outcomes matter? What outcomes do recent graduates believe they achieved and what was missing in their education? How do respondents rank or prioritize these outcomes? I often test outcomes and ask respondents to rank them via surveys and then follow up by exploring results in focus groups. For schools developing a vision of the graduate or a learning philosophy, this process can be extremely valuable.

Strategic Choices: Testing choices and new initiatives can be critical to ensuring you don't go too far down a road only to discover there was something you did not understand. For example, I worked with a boarding school that was adamant that its community wanted global offerings in the form of exchange programs and trips. They believed a global exchange for every student was a winning choice. What we learned in focus groups was surprising: parents placed low value on school-sponsored travel and higher value on exposure to global learning via curriculum and online options. Similarly, another school tested its hypothesis that all students should learn to code on computers via a survey. They learned that what the community valued for students was a macro understanding of how computers work and more knowledge of artificial intelligence and machine learning—only a small percentage of students and parents believed coding was a core skill. It became an option rather than a larger strategic choice.

Designing Surveys

Surveys should be brief and exceedingly clear in their questions. Your strategic planning committee should use the initial survey feedback in response to the one-page strategy to gather baseline data and explore reactions to vision and values. Later in your work, you can craft more specific questions to test, validate, or more deeply explore the specific strategic choices that will flow from your one-page strategy.

A school with a healthy community generally has a very high response rate. Typically, you can expect a response rate in the range of 70-90%. If you don't have a high response rate, that in and of itself is an indication that something is wrong. Your survey might have been too long, or poorly timed, or your community may be uninterested. A successful survey is one that is completed by as many people as possible, and includes only the right questions. If you have too many questions, you may lose respondents.

Design with collective intelligence and multiple perspectives. Start by forming a small team to plan, design, and test your survey. Make sure you can tap into multiple points of view and styles so that your survey is as foolproof as possible. The following checklist offers questions for discussion as you plan the survey with your design team.

Checklist #4: Ready to Design and Administer a Survey?

- What do you want your survey to signal to your community? (Excitement for the future? Desire to understand the current problems? Interest in students' needs/wants? A call for advice and input? A way to share what is aspirational or "R&D" at your school?)

- What, specifically, do you want to learn or understand? The more precise your questions with respect to what you want to know, the better.

- What do you want to test? (New ideas or initiatives, philosophical or strategic changes?)

- What do you want to measure? Are you looking for qualitative feedback that can then be quantified? Why does this data matter to your respondents?

- When do you need your data? Knowing when the data will be documented, analyzed, and presented will set the timetable for designing, sharing, and opening the survey.

- What has your school asked before? Review your previous surveys and re-ask questions to develop a longitudinal benchmark on issues central to your one-page strategy.

Consider Your Respondents and Design Accordingly

You want to ensure the highest possible response rate by considering the best conditions for that outcome. With empathy for your respondents, you can align what they need/ want with what you are trying to communicate and learn with your survey. Design with all this information at hand:

» *What will make this survey easy, compelling, and even pleasurable to complete?* Shorter surveys are always more appealing. The ideal survey takes somewhere between 5 and 15 minutes to complete, so it can be accomplished in one sitting.

» *How is your timing?* Is this a particularly busy time for respondents? Longer surveys are best reserved for periods when respondents are more likely to have time to focus. The middle of October, January, February, and April are all good times to administer surveys in school communities.

» *What about survey exhaustion?* When was the last time you asked for help? Are your constituents hungry for this opportunity, tired of requests, or somewhere in the middle? Make sure you are aware of how eager your community is and how likely they will be to participate. Communicate with other departments and divisions within your school to hold off on other surveys if need be. Strategic planning instruments should receive priority whenever possible.

» *How is your community feeling right now?* You want to ensure that your survey is not "tone deaf" to your community context. Is there something going on in your community that is causing tension, concern, and/or speculation? Will your survey be sensitive to the current climate or circumstances? Nothing is worse than surveying on a topic that seems low priority when the community is buzzing about another issue. At the same time, don't allow your team to filter all of its design through a pressing, though temporary, issue that has captured your community's attention. Address current concerns but direct your respondents to longer-term, or big picture, thinking as needed.

Formulate the Right Questions

Well-designed questions are the key to quality data. I suggest a combination of scaled questions; ranked or Yes/No responses (so you can quantify qualitative feedback); and open-ended questions (for more nuanced answers and new learning that can feed into a subsequent round of focus groups). Test your survey with a small and diverse sample of people to ensure the following:

» Questions are clear and not subject to multiple interpretations.

» Questions are not leading or suggestive.

» Questions are posed in language your community recognizes and understands.

» Questions are sensitive to the current climate and acknowledge what may be high on your community's mind.

» Questions ask respondents, when needed, to step back and examine the history and future of the school.

» Open-ended questions allow for exploration, explanation, and reframing by the respondent—what, how, and why are likely prompts.

» Close every survey with a general question to ensure room for responses you do not seek, for example: "What else would you like us to know?"

Keep Track of Your Participants

You may be surveying multiple audiences. Ideally, you want apples-to-apples data unless you are trying to research different topics with different audiences. If, for example, you are surveying parents, alumni, students, and faculty, you may wish to have a survey that asks the same questions (adjusted for the audience) with additional questions specific to each stakeholder group. You will need to include upfront a survey filter that collects profiling information in order to appropriately organize and direct the responses by category.

COMMUNITY FILTER: WHAT IS YOUR RELATIONSHIP TO THE SCHOOL?

» Current parent

» Former parent

» Faculty/Staff

» Alumni

CURRENT PARENT FILTER: WHAT GRADE IS YOUR CHILD IN?

» How many years has your child attended including this year?

» Have you had other children attend? (If yes, what year did they graduate?)

FORMER PARENT FILTER:

» When did your child (or children) graduate?

» How many years did your child attend?

ALUMNI FILTER:

» Graduation year?

» Years you attended?

FACULTY OR STAFF FILTER:

» Faculty/Staff?

» Years Working at School?

Design a Good Scale

You want your survey to feel easy to use, especially when creating your scaled questions. The scale needs to clearly indicate what you are measuring across a few indicators. I've had good success using simple, relatable language, including smiley faces or other visuals that appeal to the youngest respondents. Often these are administered in classrooms where teachers can introduce the survey, answer any questions, and collect responses on paper. Older students can use laptops in advisory or classroom settings.

» **Make each scale label clear and specific and note the spectrum (Pole to Pole or Ascending/Descending).**

» **Effective pole-to-pole scales use words like:** *Extremely Satisfied, Moderately Satisfied, Slightly Satisfied, Slightly Dissatisfied, Moderately Dissatisfied, Extremely Dissatisfied.*

» **Effective ascending/descending ranges use words like:** *Always, Frequently, Sometimes, Rarely, Never.*

» **A Note on "Neutral":** I avoid using the Neutral midpoint on a scale because I find it to be a "default position" with no real value. People who are unsure or doing the survey quickly will sometimes mark Neutral without really thinking which side of the fence they lean toward. In cases where appropriate, it is best to use **Don't Know (DK)** or **Not Applicable (NA)**, as either is more accurate.

WHAT THE EXPERTS SAY ABOUT SURVEYS

Qualtrics, a leading experiential research firm, offers the following guidelines for a good scale:

- It should be easy to interpret the meaning of each scale point.

- The meaning of scale points should be interpreted identically by all respondents.

- The scale should include enough points to differentiate respondents from one another as much as validly possible.

- Responses to the scale should be reliable, meaning that if asked the same question again, each respondent should provide the same answer.

- The scale's points should map as closely as possible to the underlying idea (construct) of the scale.

Select a Good Tool to Administer Your Survey

Survey Monkey (www.surveymonkey.com) is easy to use and offers tools to sort and analyze data. Google Forms (www.google.com/forms) is also a good choice for simple, smaller surveys. Choose the tool that offers the most ease and flexibility relative to survey design and how the data is aggregated, manipulated (cut and organized), synthesized, and presented so you can make the best use of it as quickly as possible. Any tool that converts data to text and visual presentation (think bar and pie charts) or that can code/aggregate specific types of responses (frequency of word use, for example) is also helpful.

Communicate and Share Your Survey Effectively

Assuming you will use email as your primary tool to announce and distribute the survey, include a cover letter to accompany the survey link. It is also important to consider who the survey comes from and create a strong subject line. You need to grab the attention of the addressee! An email from the Head of School/Board Chair or Strategic Planning Chair is often best.

CRAFT A SHORT BUT MEANINGFUL LETTER THAT:

» **Circles back to your original planning work.** Why does this survey matter to the respondent and to you, what do you hope to learn, and how will you use and share the data?

» **Considers the context.** Why survey now?

» **Provides clear instructions.** How long will this survey take? What is the deadline? Two weeks is an ample window to be "live." Don't hesitate to set up reminders (including a day-before-closing call to action); people are busy and a few well-timed reminders will likely increase your response rates.

» **Assures confidentiality.** How will the data be protected? If the respondent wishes to be known, or has other concerns, how can he or she reach out to you?

» Shows your gratitude. You need your community, so remind them of their value and their impact! People want to know what happens as a result of the survey and how the school utilizes the feedback. As soon as you are ready, celebrate the victories and the areas for growth as transparently as possible. Use the data to invite more involvement, support a new initiative, and frame your planning.

Sample Survey Introduction Letter

Dear SCHOOL Community,

Thank you for participating in this survey. We are interested in learning more about your experience at SCHOOL, and your interests and priorities for the school as we design our strategy for the future. This survey is entirely confidential. Your answers are submitted anonymously and will be used only for the purposes of gathering information. While the survey may look long, it should take no more than 15 minutes to complete. You will need to complete the survey in one sitting. The survey will be open until DATE.

We deeply value your thoughtful and candid responses. Your input is an essential ingredient to our process and the identification of future priorities for the school. We will share what we learn at/on MEETING TIME/DATE as we move forward in our work to develop a vision and plan for the future. If you have any questions, please contact XXX.

Thank you!

Interviewing and Focus Groups

Whether you are in a one-on-one interview or in a focus group, you will be exploring and experiencing the point of view of others. This is the key to empathy. You seek to understand, therefore you do your empathy work without judgment, inspiring an authentic response from your interviewees.

WITHIN A FOCUS GROUP, I RECOMMEND ESTABLISHING CLEAR BOUNDARIES FOR THE DIALOGUE. THE QUALITY OF THE RESEARCH DEPENDS ON CANDOR AND HONESTY. TO ENCOURAGE FORTHRIGHT COMMUNICATION, I SUGGEST SHARING THE FOLLOWING NORMS FOR FOCUS GROUPS:

» All individual statements and contributions from focus group participants are kept confidential. In our reporting, your insights and comments will never be attributed or assigned. Rather, we report in the aggregate, distilling themes, issues, concerns, and aspirations that surface. If we use quotes or report specific stories to illustrate our conclusions, we do so in ways that do not identify the person(s) to which they are attributed.

» We expect that confidentiality will be preserved by focus group participants and that they will not repeat or report anything they hear to others outside of the focus group.

Your focus groups can include students, faculty and staff, school leadership, parents, and community members, including alumni and the people in the community in which you reside. You likely have other organizations that you interact with, including neighbors and local politicians. You're going to have to decide which community members are of value to you, and what is going on in your town that will affect you.

Whether you are interviewing, focus grouping, or observing and asking questions in your school, I suggest dividing the work in steps with each of your key constituencies into excavation, probing, confirming/reframing, and elaboration. Use these four steps and sample questions to design your focus group interview script.

Step 1: Excavate. Before sharing the one-page strategy with the focus group, design and ask questions to take stock of where you are by understanding what's really happening at school today. This step is important: your focus group members should fully articulate their point of view *before* responding to the one-page strategy draft so their thoughts aren't constrained by the document, or make them feel obligated to offer supportive statements that may not fully represent their true thoughts. Without having an extensive "baseline" measure of community sentiment (one which is more thorough than your initial data collection, discussed in Chapter 2), you might spend time designing a strategy that is not aligned with your current organization's capacity. This includes where your school is, where your students are, where your teachers and staff are, what your capacity looks like, and what obstacles you need to remove in order to move to your vision. Through excavation, you may discover that students are miserable and overwhelmed, or that the faculty has no time to breathe and they're exhausted. Whatever you dig up, you'll be in a better position to understand the reactions to your initial one-page strategy.

Between the first and second steps of conducting the focus group meeting, share the draft one-page strategy with your participants. The final steps will allow you to discover how your community receives the draft, what ideas they'll offer for the next iteration, and which specific practices and programmatic changes they think should flow from the strategic choices you initially suggest.

Step 2: Probe. During the second stage of each focus group, you will invite members to connect their lived experience of the school to the one-page strategy draft. You can deepen your understanding of their current attitudes by probing why they react. What is unclear or problematic in the one-page strategy? Missing? Motivating? Exciting? Their responses will likely enrich their reflection on their current experience while giving you valuable ideas about how to improve the draft itself.

Step 3: Confirm and Reframe. Deepen and synthesize the focus group members' assessment following their reflection on the one-page strategy draft. As your interviewees put forward a challenge or note an obstacle to embracing the one-page strategy, read it back to them to confirm what you heard, and then talk with them about how else they might restate the problem so that you can understand it better. Just as important, when they embrace language from the vision, values, or strategic choices, it is important to understand why it resonated so well so you can build on those successes.

For example, a faculty member might say, "There is no time to integrate experiential learning outside of school in our curriculum." And you would repeat back, "I hear you saying there's no time for that kind of work. Can you help us understand that problem more clearly? Why do you believe there isn't time? You mentioned before you saw the draft that you have concerns about the number of expectations placed on faculty members. Are these issues related?" Here you're trying to connect their macro beliefs and the micro reactions to the strategy as you've conceived it. Not sure what to ask? Your secret weapon is a simple statement: "Tell me more." You'll discover what you need to know.

EMPATHY REFLECTIONS

- What did you hear/notice?

- What themes arose?

- What else would you like to learn?

- Who else do you need to talk to?

- How/when do we share this information with our community?

Step 4: Elaborate. I recommend ending the focus group in as concrete a way as possible so participants feel confident that they have shared actionable feedback with you. Though you want to communicate that not each and every recommendation can be incorporated, ending by recording specific feedback related to the strategic priorities or choices contained in the one-page strategy draft is a good way for your focus group members to leave feeling confident in the overall planning process.

During this step, ask your participants to suggest specific ways that they envision the strategic choices and priorities being put into practice in light of the criticism they offered. If you want your school to bring authentic learning experiences in your community into the curriculum, for example, invite your focus group members to brainstorm specific ways to use time, staff, and resources to accomplish that goal while recognizing the pressure created by, say, a recent onslaught of instructional demands.

Afterward, identify common themes or experiences and share this feedback with the broader strategic planning committee. The focus group results, along with the observational work described below, will be your bridge between the first and next draft of your strategic plan. As you move to the next drafting stage, be certain to communicate a high-level summary of your focus group findings so the community knows that their time has been valued and that each constituent group's voice continues to be valued in the planning process.

SAMPLE FOCUS GROUP QUESTIONS:

The following are suggested focus group questions for each major school constituency group, organized by the four steps described above.

» **How would you describe the educational philosophy of your school?**

» **What outcomes matter most for your school's students?**

» **What would you change about how your school thinks about learning?**

» **What are your school's strengths? Areas for improvement?**

» **What should your school focus on in the next few years?**

Focus Group Your Administrative Team

EXCAVATE	PROBE	CONFIRM/ REFRAME	ELABORATE
How would you describe the dynamic within your leadership team?

How do you set goals and how effectively have you managed progress toward those goals?

With which of the following groups do you have the best relationship? The worst?

• Faculty?

• Students?

• Parents? | Which parts of the one-page strategy would receive strong support from a broad consensus of the school? Which would push the school in ways that may be perceived as challenging or misguided?

How confident are you in communicating the vision and values captured in the current strategy draft?

How confident are you in your team's management capacity to execute the strategic goals listed herein? What do you need to help? | How do choices made in the one-page strategy play to your existing strengths? What capacities would you need to build in order to make the strategy a reality?

What lingering concerns are you now willing to address in order to adopt and act on this version of the strategic plan? What do you need to alter given your team's current leadership capacity? | What specific program and practice changes would you want to see or avoid in order to act on the strategic choices listed in the one-page draft?

Which specific steps would be embraced or resisted? By whom? Does that change your opinion about which specific changes should come first? |

Focus Group Your Faculty/Staff

EXCAVATE	PROBE	CONFIRM/ REFRAME	ELABORATE
How would you describe the school climate? How do leadership, parents, or students impact the climate?	Which parts of the one-page strategy can you most easily visualize existing in your school? Which seems most foreign?	How would parents and students support or resist implementing key elements of the draft one-page strategy?	Imagine specific practices and program changes you would like to see first, based on the strategic choices described in this draft? Which would you like to see a little later?
How do teachers collaborate?	Which parts speak to why you are a teacher/ staff member?	Would you have confidence in the ability of admin to implement this plan well?	Which specific steps would excite faculty? Could alleviate existing issues?
How do teachers grow and learn about best teaching practices?	Which parts will be the easiest or most difficult to implement and why?	Would the short-term challenges be worth the long-term benefits of implementing the vision, values, and choices described in this draft?	

Focus Group Your Students

EXCAVATE	PROBE	CONFIRM/ REFRAME	ELABORATE
Why do students choose your school?	Which parts of the one-page strategy draft capture your life inside classrooms? Outside of classrooms?	If the school changed along the lines suggested in this plan, would student life improve significantly for you?	What are the specific changes you would like to see the school make as suggested by the strategic priorities and plans at the end of the draft?
What do you love about your school? What don't you like? What issues do students talk about?	Which parts of the vision or values express how students feel about your school?	Do you think the school could successfully adopt or practice the ideas listed in this draft? Why or why not?	What changes would make your experience more rewarding now? In the future?
How are your connections with adults at your school?	Which parts capture how you wish to feel about your school?		
(For upper-year students) What will you miss when you leave? What will you not miss?			

Focus Group Your Parents

EXCAVATE	PROBE	CONFIRM/ REFRAME	ELABORATE
How much do your children enjoy attending your school?	Which parts of the draft strategy memo capture your aspirations for your children? Which capture why you chose to join this school?	Do you feel that the administration is prepared to live out the priorities articulated in the draft strategy memo? The faculty?	What specific changes would you like to see based on the strategic priorities and choices listed at the end of the one-page draft?
What are interactions like between parents and leadership? Between parents and faculty?	Which represent changes you would like to see at your school?	Do you feel that students would be better prepared after graduation if the school met these priorities? Would they be happier at school now?	What would you want to see done first to implement the priorities? What would you not want to see happen?
What issues do parents talk about the most? What issues do school leaders talk to you about the most?	Which represent changes most parents would like to see?		
What would you like to see leadership focus on in the next 3–5 years?	What challenges do you foresee in living up to the commitments made in this draft?		

Focus Group Your Alumni

EXCAVATE	PROBE	CONFIRM/ REFRAME	ELABORATE
How does the school interact with its alumni?	Which parts of the draft strategy memo best reflect your memories of your school experience? What is your sense of the school today?	How would the reputation of the school change if it adopted the draft strategy memo?	Which specific changes in program and practice would you recommend?
What inspires you to remain connected to your school? What tends to discourage your connection?		Would you be more or less likely to send your child to your *alma mater* if it adopted this draft strategy? Why?	Which would have the biggest impact on your opinion of the school and its reputation in your community?
How do people react when they learn you attended this school?	If the school committed to the vision, values, and priorities, how would your engagement with the school change?		
What do you value the most about your experience at the school? What do you regret about your experience?			

Observations: Learning Walks and Shadowing

One of my favorite forms of research is what I call "learning walks." The GLP team will visit a school and in a relaxed way walk around, peeking into classrooms, cafeterias, sports fields, student centers, faculty lounges, etc. As we tour about, we ask questions, being careful to maintain our empathetic approach—no judgment, just listening to understand. We engage kids and adults simply to take in the energy of the school. Do people seem happy? Engaged? Confident? Interested? Rushing about? Bored? Tired or stressed? Observations lead to informal interviews and conversations in which we can probe what we see. And, as we observe, we document, reflect upon, and test our observations. Then we return to see if what we initially observed is evident all the time, or just an outlier observation. It helps to have an outsider do this work, but an insider, carefully chosen, can do it with greater frequency and depth. At this stage, you can conduct your own learning walks to validate or raise questions about commitments expressed in your draft one-page strategy. How far are you from the aspirations and strategic choices in your draft?

Another effective way to observe how elements of your one-page strategy would relate to the current school culture is to "shadow" a student or a colleague. What's it like to live the life of a ninth grader for an entire day? What's it like to live in the shoes of your Head of School? What do you notice? What can you learn about the culture and climate of your school? Switch roles, and ask Trustees, staff, and teachers to shadow students or colleagues and document and discuss their observations.

Incorporating a shadowing experience to explore key issues raised in your one-page strategy is a terrific way to get both qualitative and quantitative data and raise awareness and excitement about the planning process itself. For instance, at the Latin School of Chicago, faculty completed over two-dozen shadowing days over the span of two years from grades Junior Kindergarten-12. Using Latin's standard student shadowing observation template (reproduced here) faculty recorded opportunities for students to move, choose their activity, collaborate, and meaningfully participate. They also tracked the share of time students were expected to use a device in their work and stress levels throughout the day. Supplemented by a homework log and student interviews, the shadowing program informed the school's Wellness Committee priorities and helped Latin communicate to its constituents the renewed focus it was placing on student well-being.

Figure 1. Shadowing Worksheet

CLASS: TIME: TEACHER:

Homework assigned:

Transition into class: Calm? Rushed? Opportunity to reflect/consolidate previous session?

Record your observation every 10 minutes. If you have a long block, use extra sheet for final 4 notes.

DESCRIBE CLASSROOM ACTIVITY	DESCRIPTION OF MOOD, ENERGY, ENJOYMENT	OPPORTUNITIES PROVIDED BY TEACHERS	STUDENT BEHAVIORS	ASSORTED NOTES:
		To move? To participate? To collaborate? To choose task?	Moved Participated Collaborated Chose own activity Screen time	
		To move? To participate? To collaborate? To choose task?	Moved Participated Collaborated Chose own activity Screen time	
		To move? To participate? To collaborate? To choose task?	Moved Participated Collaborated Chose own activity Screen time	
		To move? To participate? To collaborate? To choose task?	Moved Participated Collaborated Chose own activity Screen time	
		To move? To participate? To collaborate? To choose task?	Moved Participated Collaborated Chose own activity Screen time	Was Homework addressed?

Transition at end of class: Calm? Rushed? Opportunity to reflect/consolidate this session?

Observer estimate of student stress: Not at all _____   A little _____   Some _____   Quite a bit _____   A lot _____

Observer estimate of student engagement: Not at all _____   A little _____   Some _____   Quite a bit _____   A lot _____

Follow up questions for student:

EXERCISE: **DRAWING EXERCISES**

In the effort to engage members of all ages and of different preferred communication styles in reflecting on the draft one-page strategy, visual and creative exercises are terrific ways to describe experiences and convey emotions without the challenge of conversations. For some people, these exercises are the best way to express what they want or how they experience school.

Damian Bebell, an Assistant Research Professor at Boston College's Lynch School of Education, taught us how to use drawing exercises to help understand the hopes and aspirations of students for the school experience. By coding those drawings, you can actually quantify their experience.

Develop your own hypotheses about what you expect to see captured in the drawings. Discovering a gap between the assumptions or expectations embodied in your one-page strategy and the content of the pictures can be very revealing.

DRAWING PROMPTS:

> Think about the teachers and the kinds of things you do in your classrooms. Draw a picture of one of your teachers working in his or her classroom.

> Think about the kinds of work and activities you do in your classes. Draw a picture of what a camera would see when you are learning in the classroom.

> Think about the teachers and the kinds of things you have done in your class today. Draw a picture of your teacher teaching and yourself learning.

- Draw a picture of yourself taking the "big test."

- Think about the math work and activities you do outside of school. Draw a picture of yourself learning math outside of school.

- Think about the work and activities you do in math class. Draw a picture of yourself learning math in school.

Collect the drawings. Look for indicators suggested by your hypotheses and begin to notice repeated characteristics or elements in drawings as you review the data. The indicators should track behaviors you aspire to see (or avoid), or that you already promote (or avoid), as articulated in the one-page strategy statement. Once you've identified characteristics or elements, you can assign each a category label, and then begin to "code" each drawing. You can account for the frequency/percentage of times certain characteristics or elements are present in a group of drawings.

For each drawing exercise, reflect on the following:

- What patterns do you see in the drawings?

- Why do you think these patterns occur?

- How did the patterns you discover diverge from or confirm your hypotheses?

- What do you think might be done differently in your school as a result of what you see in the drawings?

NOTES: RECORD WHAT YOU LEARNED

EXERCISE: **IDEAL EXPERIENCE**

I once did this exercise with a client developing an after-school program: I asked the students to draw their ideal experience, and over 85 percent of the drawings had outdoor elements and spaces to play. This information helped the client realize that the children needed more movement, playtime, and outdoor experiences. The school moved quickly to redesign programming to ensure physical activity, outdoor experiences, and unstructured time to play.

Depending on your one-page strategy and the questions asked, you may want to identify and quantify indicators of the current experience that signal what students feel and how they engage with their environment.

Examples of elements to "code":

» Students working in groups

» Students seated in rows

» Teacher placement

» Facial expressions

» Windows

» Plants (or books, or soft furniture)

» Sunshine

» Diverse activities among students and/or adults

» Environmental elements

You'll make some pretty quick assessments with these drawings, but you'll also identify areas for deeper exploration—and your faculty will have data that can help them design for the future.

NOTES: RECORD WHAT YOU LEARNED

Case Study: Indian Mountain School

Indian Mountain, a junior boarding school in Connecticut with a strong history and traditions, wanted to clarify its core values as part of its strategic design work. I suggested that they invite some students into the conversation. The strategic planning committee invited a couple of their older students to speak with them about the school's values and discuss where the school is going. Jody Soja, the Head of School wrote in an update to her families:

> Each of the four students on the committee spoke about how their experience at IMS has shaped them. They feel courageous, encouraged to step outside their comfort zones to try new things. They have strong relationships with supportive teachers, understand how to live and learn in a community while making meaningful contributions to it, and wish for more integration of students in different divisions. Hearing these students, a vocal and opinionated group of adults went quiet, more than a few reaching for a tissue. This is what IMS is about.

One idea that came from Indian Mountain School students was a pervasive culture of courage. Many of the students were leaving home at a young age, and some were coming from outside the United States. The students believed that they learned courage at school, with their peers, and working with the faculty and staff. Had the kids not been included in that conversation, the team would not have hit on that point of what was really important to them.

Following the empathy work, the cornerstone of courage became one of IMS's core values. Understanding this re-engaged the committee and helped the members to reframe their sense of vision and mission. They connected the value of courage to the opportunities they had for outdoor education on the mountain, and they adopted the notion of "the courage to climb" as being both a metaphor and a literal statement that they could use for learning within their community. Courage became a galvanizing idea, not only as a value, but as an inspiration and a lens through which they would think about learning for everybody. As a result, their strategic design became dramatically more precise, clear, and relevant.

Notes:

DESIGN AND TEST

Strategic design drives fresh thinking and results, but only through a thoughtful process that empowers people to act. Now that you've established a dialogue with students, faculty, staff, parents, and/or alumni, it is time to synthesize what you've learned from their reflections on the draft one-page strategy, build on suggestions that emerged, and ask different people for further help in designing solutions. It's time to act.

First, everyone needs feedback about what emerged in your work to empathize with the many perspectives inside your school community. What themes arose as you listened and learned? How does what you learned help define the problems and frame the opportunities you want to tackle? What obstacles exist in the work? At this point in the process, it may be helpful to talk with leadership to pin down values-based non-negotiables or practical constraints you may have in your design process. For example, what resources, limitations, or restrictions must now be on the table as you begin to clarify your strategic choices and design the "how" of strategy?

Second, you'll use the feedback to refine and revise your working vision and the emerging choices within your one-page strategy design. You may also have a clearer definition of your values. With this next iteration of your strategic design, you now have the "frame" and you can turn back to your colleagues to "paint the picture within." You will design, experiment with, and test strategic choices and specific goals you might pursue in service of those choices, with the people who are actually executing and impacted by the work. By the end of this chapter, your one-page strategy will have morphed from a draft to a more fully thought out road map with goals, action items, and execution steps.

Design Thinking, Part Two

Your design is evolving and now you are ready to test the how and what of strategic execution. Let's recap the elements:

Define

The define mode brings deeper clarity and focus to your work. You will be defining the challenge (or opportunity) you are taking on, based on what you have learned during your empathy work for the initial draft of the one-page strategy.

A design challenge is a way to rethink or invent a practice, product, or program in order to create better outcomes in your school. Within your strategic design, each choice will suggest design challenges. For example, you may have a choice that commits to redesigning how you use time to deepen and enrich the learning experiences. One challenge may be expressed in the question: "How do we reimagine the academic calendar and daily schedule so we can do more project-based, trans-disciplinary work; offer adults more time to collaborate and design; and build in internship or expeditionary experiences for students?"

It often helps to choose specific questions to move through the process and build your capacity for this kind of work. As a foundation to defining problems, it can be helpful to first identify the gaps and the strong alignments between your values and the ways in which your school operates. By talking about the actual practices, policies, and behaviors of your school today, you can begin to get more specific about what to eliminate, innovate, or adapt in order to operationalize the commitments in the newest iteration of your one-page strategy.

ORGANIZATIONAL ALIGNMENT EXERCISE:
STOP, CONTINUE, START FOR TEACHERS & STUDENTS

After receiving feedback on the one-page strategy and completing the needed revisions, you can begin to define which problems you see arising around the design question posed by the goals expressed in the one-page strategy. Let's continue with an example challenge of promoting project-based learning in the face of a traditional academic calendar. You may need to test some assumptions—this time with the people who execute. Why do we teach in singular disciplines or in blocks between 8am and 2pm? Why do we hold school from September to May? Why does all school currently happen in school? You'll need leadership to guide you as to what's on and off the table, but the key is to give yourself a blank slate for this part of the thinking!

The following exercise helps you explore how practices, behaviors, and policies in your school act in service of your proposed core values and where opportunities exist to change, eliminate, and create new ways of doing things. In order to avoid groupthink, make sure that within each group time is given at the outset for individual reflection on these questions. Then, ask each person to share his or her ideas within each category. Post this protocol clearly for members to see.

I often use this exercise with students and faculty/staff groups to learn more about the realities of the school experience. If you sense dissonance in your organization—lower than expected faculty morale, increasingly challenging parents—then there's likely a disconnect between what you value and what you actually do.

Divide your group of teachers and/or students into smaller teams of between five and ten members. Recommend that each group appoint a recorder who will take notes in a manner that can be easily shared. Begin by reviewing together the core values of the school. Then ask each group to think about the practices, programs, or policies that align or do not align with core values.

Next, ask the group to develop a list of practices, policies, or programs that they would like to Stop, Continue, or Start:

1. What at your school would you STOP doing?

2. What at your school would you CONTINUE doing?

3. What at your school would you START or innovate?

NOTES: RECORD WHAT YOU LEARNED

It is always hardest to come up with what you will *stop* doing, but this is a critical piece of information to successfully focus your organization on those strategic choices that best further your values, vision, and mission. This is the first step to avoiding the trap that so many independent schools find themselves in: adding programming (and demands on time) to existing teacher and student commitments without acknowledging trade-offs, the need for values alignment, and the potential effect on community wellness.

After executing this activity with faculty, staff and students, you've likely identified practices and programs that are or are not aligned with the emerging vision and values of your school, as well as what students and faculty would want to begin in order to implement that vision and values. This is a good time to consult the Board's work on what to leverage and build from in their earlier work so you can engage them in discussion of how best to manage the school's assets in furtherance of those goals. Each of the stop/start/continue recommendations represents an opportunity, but not all of them can be acted upon because of limited resources and the need to stagger initiatives in a sustainable manner. You'll need a more precise definition of the most important problem(s) your one-page strategy is trying to address, and filter all the recommendations you generated in the previous two exercises through that screen.

How do you identify the best problems or opportunities to focus on? This is the time to clarify even further what you are trying to solve and discuss the implications of what you agree to tackle. Sometimes there are many problems tangled up together— schedule, contracts, parent expectations—and it is hard to identify the root cause or the underlying issue you need to examine. I suggest using a process of hypothesizing possibilities so you can discuss what makes most sense:

> » Craft a meaningful and actionable problem statement that contains a theory of change. Develop if, then statements: *IF we do X ... THEN we can achieve Y*. Be clear to yourself what cause/effect story drives the change you'll make to solve the problem.

> » Remember that at this stage you are not solving the problem, you are simply identifying the right one to tackle. For example: "If we are willing to think about the calendar year as one that includes twelve months, we can create time and space for all the things we want to design for learners—adults and students!"

» Further refine your understanding of the problem with a question or two that builds on your hypothesis. To continue the example: How might we create meaningful time for project-based learning in the school day/week/semester if we imagine our year over twelve months? How might we test the impact of blending disciplines and designing projects on teacher planning time? As you explore these questions, and the new possibilities that surface, you'll get closer to identifying a specific area on which to focus your intervention or innovation.

NOTES: RECORD WHAT YOU LEARNED

Ideate

The next element in the process is when you concentrate on idea generation. Ideation provides both the fuel and the source material for building prototypes and finding innovative solutions. You will be discussing potential ways to address a single issue. Keep it generative and use Post-it notes to capture individual voices and group discussions.

Ideation Activities: Brainstorming!

» Now that we have defined the problem through our hypothesis and results of the stop/start/continue exercise, what ideas do we have to solve it? Have everyone participating write down as many ideas as they can come up with on Post-it notes to share with the group.

» No evaluation! This should be fun and free-flowing. Build on each other's ideas—however wild, outlandish, or humorous. Some of the best solutions come from "bad" initial ideas that offer seeds of inspiration.

» Each member of the group should write down their own thoughts; there should be no designated recorder who filters individual ideas.

» The team should be moving, or at least standing, while interacting. Sitting breeds passivity and narrow thinking.

» Pose initial constraints at the outset if it helps focus your imagination a bit. For example: we will design only with ideas that are no-cost or low-cost, or not a programmatic addition, or don't require a new hire, etc.

» Converge in any way that makes sense—first within your own group, and then, if applicable, across many groups. You'll have at least one if not more ideas, which you can now prototype!

NOTES: RECORD WHAT YOU LEARNED

Prototype

The prototype mode is the space for building samples/experiments in service of implementing elements of your revised one-page strategy that are quick and cheap to make (think minutes and cents) but can solicit useful feedback. A prototype can be anything that a user can interact with—be it a wall of Post-it notes, a gadget you put together, a role-playing activity, or even a storyboard. A prototype can also be a short-term or small-scale, but real, version of something you'd like to pursue—a one-day or one-week experiment. Depending on the size of the group you are engaging in this process, you can either develop one prototype to test or break up the group into smaller teams that will each develop their own prototype and bring it back to the group. The second option allows you to take the best ideas from each of the prototypes and combine them for a final prototype. Either way, you want to keep the needs of the end user in mind as you add details to your vision.

I love to combine professional learning with the prototype mode by constructing it as a project for adults, in the same way we as educators do for students. The benefits are multiple: adults get to learn by working on real issues for their school; they are empowered to create solutions they can implement; the school builds in time and resources for true R&D; speakers or resources can be blended to directly align with what you are trying to accomplish; and so forth. Best of all, prototyping reduces the risks of wholesale change by localizing and scaling down an innovation to ensure its value. Prototypes allow for experimentation that doesn't force you to "throw the baby out with the bathwater."

PROTOTYPE ACTIVITIES:

» **Agree on a design prototype: What are we going to do? Why?**

» **Develop a design prototype and plan: How are we going to do it? With whom? When?**

» **Prepare for exhibition: How are we going to share our design prototype and plan?**

» Questions to consider:

- Have we answered the key design questions in developing our prototype: who, what, why, when, how?

- Which elements of ideas and prototype suggestions can we use in formulating our first best design?

- How can we measure our prototype within a set period of time?

NOTES: RECORD WHAT YOU LEARNED

DESIGN THINKING BEYOND STRATEGIC DESIGN

You can use design thinking to rethink how you hold faculty meetings and/or professional development retreats, how teams form and organize, or how you make decisions. The formula is flexible, so be creative and use the modes in ways that best suit the challenge before you.

Test

The test mode is when you solicit feedback about your prototype. This is another opportunity to gain empathy information. A rule of thumb: always prototype as if you know you're right, but test as if you know you're wrong. Testing is the chance to refine your solutions, poke holes in your thinking, and discover the unanticipated impacts of your design. Testing helps to reveal how you can improve your design going forward.

I also encourage that you design with an eye to assessment so you have some idea of which evidence you'll need to know how your design works. For example, if a key strategic choice in your one-page strategy is to promote greater community integration, and you are designing a new experience for transitioning and orienting new ninth graders to school, you might be interested in knowing that students connected successfully with a supportive adult, learned how to navigate the school, felt welcomed and included, and so forth. The assessment might be a survey and/or focus group with these same students to find out how they responded to the experience based on the outcomes you hoped to achieve.

Assessments should be quantitative or qualitative, depending on what you're designing. Make sure you prototype with enough time to collect enough information to assess your experiment effectively. For example, a one-day schedule experiment may not be enough to understand the impact over the course of a week or marking period. How can you simulate the most comprehensive context for understanding a proposed change?

You can reflect on your test by creating yet another feedback loop to the stakeholders for whom this will matter: perhaps it is the Board, parents, or your faculty and staff. When you present the plan, tell the story of your process. Don't forget to remind the community about how you got there. Celebrate the process, honor their involvement, and document your learning. And keep doing this work—you don't need a formal planning process to ask for feedback!

There are a few likely scenarios that can occur in the testing stage. When you converge back with your team, you either report that the test went great and you've decided that you're moving forward, or the test failed or surfaced some discrepancies that you then address in the next iteration of your strategic design.

Case Study: Miss Hall's School

A small girls' boarding school, whose mission is to prepare girls with a strong a sense of self and the agency to make a difference in the world, wanted to build a strategy that actively engaged students in the strategic design process. The new Head of School was very committed to empowering the students in the process as a way to authentically live into their mission.

The school facilitated a range of visioning, design thinking exercises, empathy, and "stop/start/continue" exercises. The school worked closely with students to develop strategic choices that framed issues, opportunities, and easy solutions that would have gone unrecognized without the active participation of students.

Students wanted to protect and build upon a palpable sense of joy and close relationships that they believed constituted the foundation of their school community. Adults realized that the best conditions for learning for their students were grounded in a culture and environment where students were accepted, respected, and encouraged to grow into their identities as young adults. The students felt that the seeds were there but that there were aspects of the program and residential experience that could be redesigned for even greater impact. This choice—to emphasize joy and community—became a centerpiece of the strategic design and a deep source of pride for the entire school. It became a unique and compelling element of the value proposition and brand, which then could be carried through to a coherent approach for program and pedagogical development.

The Next Step

You are in the home stretch and getting close to planting your flag on the mountaintop that describes strategy! Remember, you've worked through a process to listen and learn, to surface values, develop vision, hone in on strategic choices, and articulate it all on one page. Now you need to reassure yourself that you are ready to commit: you'll take educated risks, focus resources and efforts, build the culture you want, and execute with coherence and shared purpose.

Notes:

MAKE CHOICES AND BUILD COMMITMENT

....

In this chapter, you're going to go back to your team and review the results of your empathetic conversations (Chapter 6) and testing of prototype reforms (Chapter 7) inspired by your one-page strategy draft. You'll begin to plan execution so you can present your strategy with confidence to your Board and to your community. You are now ready to make some choices and express them with greater precision. If we return to the mountain metaphor, now that you've done some preliminary exploration and scouting, it is time to determine which trails might be the best ones to take.

Strategic choices define the key decisions you make: they are visionary statements about your intentions. You've made real headway in seeing these for your school. Now, for everyone to understand what they mean, you'll want to explore and describe the "on the dance floor" implications—naming potential goals and tactics that describe the "how" of these strategic choices.

Creating Schools That Thrive: A Blueprint for Strategy

In your focus groups from Chapter 6, you invited community members to think about the concrete implications of your strategic goals. You don't need to map every step of implementation (and you shouldn't) but you will need to give everyone an opportunity to consider what these choices mean in terms of the nuts and bolts of execution. You'll also need ways to solve problems as you move through this work, and as you track and assess your progress. Finally, you'll need to affirm or adapt your mission and then present your design for formal adoption by the Board.

Link Strategy to Execution: Design Goals and Tactics

Your work to this point has revealed some key next steps: you may have named what needs to be further explored, what you hope to create, or what is already in process (prototyped) that you are going to continue to further test and refine. These are your goals and tactics. You can return to your one-page strategy now and fill in the two or three goals and tactics you'll need to fulfill each strategic choice. For instance, if you've already tested a week of project-based learning, and it was well received by students and staff, you might now move to integrate it more deeply into the program. You will map how to move from "project week" to deeper project work across the learning experience.

Outlining goals and tactics continues to be "messy" work. Don't be surprised to find that there are different points of view or even deep disagreements about what steps to take first and how to assure people of their efficacy. You'll need to continue to problem-solve, collaborate, measure progress, and make decisions with the people closest to the action: those who will execute this work. This work is dynamic and ongoing, but requires discipline and structure. Two of the most useful tools are protocols (for problem solving) and dashboards (for monitoring progress).

Harness Protocols to Problem-Solve

I learned about protocols in my work with High Tech High, an exemplary network of charter schools in San Diego, California. I've adopted the protocol as a highly effective tool for schools that are trying to problem-solve, solicit feedback, or break down a problem as they design strategy. A protocol in strategic design is a structured and methodical process that fosters focused, solutions-oriented dialogue in a structure that mitigates circular or unproductive discourse. As you move toward making decisions, protocols help you harness collective intelligence to iron out differences or evaluate concrete options and plans of action in a structured format.

Protocols have a wide array of applications. For example, imagine that you've identified in strategic design that you don't use time well as an organization and you need to collaborate more effectively. You spend a lot of time in meetings and many leaders, faculty, and staff find themselves in overlapping sessions. These meetings chew up too much time, exhaust people, and feel somewhat unproductive. You want to redesign the whole process for how you meet as a team.

To get started, you can use a protocol. You'll gather key people together, appoint a facilitator, and proceed to talk about the specific challenge. Perhaps you decide to start by talking about the regular leadership meetings. Your Head of School presents the problem:

> I need to gather people together on a regular basis but we've acknowledged through our initial stages of strategic design that we are not using our time well, and many people feel like we're meeting too frequently, or in too many different places. We need to figure out how to run these meetings differently. We want to free up time to work smarter and collaborate more effectively.

The protocol is a structured process for tackling this problem. Once it is presented, the protocol group has an opportunity to ask clarifying and probing questions of the presenter that helps them understand the issue more deeply:

» **What are the most important things we need to do in our meetings?**

» **What is most frustrating about how meetings happen now?**

» **Why do we meet at these times?**

Creating Schools That Thrive: A Blueprint for Strategy

» **How are other times of the day currently used?**

» **How are agendas currently developed?**

From there, set a timer for the group to discuss the problem, consider options, and identify ways to move forward. They'll discuss this openly in a fishbowl format with the person who presented the problem stepping back to listen closely to the dialogue.

The final step is to come back together to converge and decide how you're going to move forward. Because the process is timed and facilitated, it drives the conversation and moves you toward an outcome or request for feedback that has been presented at the outset. You will need a facilitator and a presenting team or individual who describes the issue, problem, or initiative to be discussed.

Protocol Guidelines

Adapted from the Presentation of Learning Protocol
from High Tech High's Educational Leadership Academy

Appoint a Facilitator and a Documenter

It is usually easiest to separate these responsibilities. The facilitator ensures adherence to norms and process while also acting as timekeeper. The documenter takes notes, ideally in a format that is visible to all.

Establish Norms

Use norms that are right for your school or situation. Here is a sample I often use, from Rob Riordan of High Tech High:

- Be hard on the content, soft on the people

- Share the air (or "step up, then step back")

- Be kind, specific, and helpful

Conduct the Protocol

Design a timetable that fits with your context; the suggestions here are offered as samples. I recommend that a protocol be conducted within a range of 30 to 60 minutes.

The facilitator guides the discussion according to the outline below and provides corrective feedback. Don't forget to assign a timekeeper or set a timer.

Overview (10 min.)

- Ask the presenter or a presenting team to give an overview of their issue, plan, or problem.

  » Background and context.

  » Objectives, outcomes, and intentions.

  » Specific request for feedback: What would you like help with?

  » The facilitator writes this question/focus on the whiteboard or chart paper. The group may choose to use a visual to document their thinking and their vision.

Questions (10 min.)

- The facilitator provides the opportunity for the protocol group to ask clarifying and probing questions of the presenter(s) to help them better understand the issue at hand, and expand their knowledge of the facts and the point of view of the presenter.

- *Clarifying Questions* are fact finding and provide additional information for understanding content. *Probing Questions* are more open-ended and exploratory in order to learn more about intentions and interests.

- Within the window for asking questions, there should be separate times for Clarifying and Probing questions.

- The presenters respond to the group's questions, but there is no discussion at this time by the protocol group.

- Questions should not be "advice in disguise," such as "Have you considered …?" or "why wouldn't you …?" Limit questions to learning rather than suggesting or analyzing at this point in the process. The facilitator corrects participants as needed.

Discussion (10 min.)

- The facilitator asks the presenter to reframe the issue/question/feedback focus (if necessary) and then to step back from the group.

- The facilitator allows the group to discuss the issue and offer its analysis, ideas, and advice. The facilitator should ensure that the group continues to pay particular attention to the feedback focus/question(s) raised by the presenting team. The presenter does not speak during the discussion, but listens and take notes.

- It is a good idea for the presenting team to sit outside of the circle of discussion to observe. This allows the discussion group to close in and focus on each other.

- The facilitator asks everyone to begin with warm feedback/celebrations, such as "What are the strengths of this design?" or "I appreciate/admire how…"

- The facilitator next asks for cool feedback, which includes a more critical analysis of the work, using the question proposed by the presenter to frame the discussion. For example, "What isn't the presenter considering?" or "I wonder what would happen if …"

- The facilitator should try to synthesize and paraphrase feedback wherever helpful: "Given what we are hearing, it sound like there is an opportunity to …"

- The facilitator helps participants resist the urge to speak directly to the presenting team.

- The facilitator may need to remind participants of the presenters' feedback focus/questions. It can be helpful to ask after 3 minutes, "Are we addressing the presenters' questions?"

Response and Next Steps (5 min.)

- The facilitator invites the presenter or presenting team to return to the group and responds to the discussion.

    » It is not necessary to respond point by point to what others said.

    » The presenters may share what struck them and what next steps might be taken as a result of the ideas generated by the discussion.

    » The discussion group is silent.

- The facilitator asks presenters to discuss their commitment to next steps, noting what changes and adjustments they will consider making to their action plans based on the feedback. What do they need to learn more about? How will they make changes?

Debrief (5 min.)

After all the teams in the group have had a chance to present their action plans, all participants will debrief the effectiveness of the protocol.

- The facilitator leads a conversation about the group's observation of the process.

- Questions posed by the facilitator to the group might include:

    » How helpful were our questions?

    » How well did we stick to the areas of feedback focus?

    » When was a moment when a conversation made a turn for the better?

    » Was there any point where we went off track?

    » In what ways did our probing questions really push the thinking of the presenter?

- Resist the urge to turn the debrief into a discussion of the dilemma.

Tips for the Facilitator:

- Work with the presenting team to frame a good question in advance. Discuss the dilemma and wordsmith a question that is open-ended and not easily solved. Write the question on the whiteboard so that it is visible during the entire conversation.

- Stick to the timing for each section. If you need help with keeping time, ask for a volunteer to monitor it and/or use a timer.

- Don't be afraid to keep the group focused on the protocol. If a probing question is asked during clarifying questions, gently ask the participant to write it down and wait until the group has moved to that point in the conversation. If advice in disguise is offered, ask to reframe the question in a way that seeks to learn something about the presenting group's dilemma.

- Redirect the conversation when necessary (but without unnecessarily monopolizing airtime!). For example, if the discussion jumps to cool feedback before warm feedback is shared, make sure time is taken to celebrate the work first.

- Resist the urge to skip the debrief. This is a crucial way to deconstruct the conversation and improve the quality of your dialogue with colleagues over time.

- Be courageous and confident. Strong facilitation is the key to having successful dialogue about our work and is appreciated by everyone in the group. If it helps to literally read each step to the group, by all means do so.

Track Progress with Dashboards

Making programmatic commitments and living them requires learning and agility. And you can't adapt successfully if you are not thinking first about how to get the work done and then reflecting on your progress. It will also be easier to engage your Board and other key people in supporting a strategy in which you have mapped out the early stages of execution and given thought to how you'll assess and measure. As you fill in the specific programs and reforms under the strategic choices identified in your one-page strategy and get ready to adopt the plan you're crafting, be ready to offer some early execution and assessment approaches. I have provided two templates you can adapt for use while taking either the perspective of the balcony or the dance floor. You'll do the implementation plan for the step-by-step execution work internally; and you'll use the scorecard to assess progress on the one-page strategy.

Dashboard Example: GLP Implementation Plan Template

Once you have your one-page strategy well articulated, you can use a spreadsheet like the one shown below, or project management software (such as Slack or Basecamp) to break down the steps and associated roles, responsibilities, deliverables, and timelines that get you to your goals. This is an internal document for the school and it should be managed, updated, and active. The cover sheet features the vision statement, strategic choices or priorities, and the key goals. You'll detail action items, products (or deliverables), and a timeline. Then you can add the players involved and notes about progress.

For example, a key strategic choice in your plan might be to change the school day schedule, but what comes underneath that goal are the action steps: convening the task force, the date and people responsible, and the status. Add dates for reviewing the current schedule and visiting schools with different schedules. Expect to update and revise this document regularly: it is a work in progress.

Figure 2. Strategic Implementation Plan

VISION STATEMENT   RESPONSIBILITY   JUN-18   JUL-18   AUG-18   SEP-18   OCT-18   NOV-18   DEC-18   JAN-19   FEB-19

PRIORITY 1

A   Goal 1

B   Goal 2

C   Goal 3

D   Goal 4

Notes:

PRIORITY 2

A   Goal 1

B   Goal 2

C   Goal 3

D   Goal 4

Notes:

PRIORITY 3

A   Goal 1

B   Goal 2

C   Goal 3

Notes:

PRIORITY 4

A   Goal 1

B   Goal 2

C   Goal 3

Notes:

PRIORITY 5

A   Goal 1

B   Goal 2

Notes:

Example: Board/Leadership Tracking

For tracking and discussing progress at the leadership level (the leadership team) you may want to roll up to a higher-level dashboard that directly reflects your one-page strategy. It's a useful tool for leadership updates. With your Board, you'll want to regularly update the dashboard and discuss it deeply at least quarterly. With your team, you should determine what's urgent, what's important, and what's working well around the areas of implementation. This dashboard is designed to track progress in a way that is clear, easy, and visually accessible.

As you prepare for implementation, you need to decide how you will measure progress toward your strategic goals. I have found that there are six key questions you need to answer in designing your dashboard. You need to develop a strategically informed screen to determine which of the many possible concepts you could measure. You need to identify a limited set of measures so you retain your strategic focus, and orient and educate your community about the meaning and significance of each one.

Question 1: What does educational research tell you about the relation between your strategic choices and key outcomes? What is the cause and effect story that connects your strategic choices and improvements in student and school performance?

Each element of your dashboard should be founded on a research-based hypothesis that connects your changes in program and practice to outcomes.

Question 2: How do the elements of your dashboard fit together to reflect the mission, vision, and values of your school? Together, how do the dashboard measures tell a unique story of who you are?

To the limited extent that dashboards exist for schools, they are tilted toward standardized academic testing data, GPAs, or college placements because these are easy to collect and readily available. Don't let the immediacy of access to such data misshape your dashboard if you are also committed to social emotional growth or twenty-first century skills that are captured by different measures.

How will your set of dashboard measures capture both where your school is now and where it is going?

Select a balance of lagging indicators that reflect the accumulated impact of previous practice and programs, and leading indicators that suggest progress toward your goals. This will allow you to mark longitudinal progress over time (lagging) but also communicate that you are fulfilling promises now (leading) that will cash out in improvements according to the hypotheses you make explicit in response to Question 1.

How will you evaluate your performance? How will you know if the plan is going well?

Whenever possible, selecting measures with peer benchmarks is vital. Peer benchmarks maintain accountability, educate your Board and parents, and offer rich opportunities for enrollment management and development messaging. Consult your accrediting association, NAIS, and INDEX (www.indexgroups.org) for available benchmark measures and data. Though each school is certainly unique, developing a consistent set of dashboard measures is essential for reliable longitudinal benchmarks (Chapter 9 will review formulating your dashboard).

What incentives are you introducing to the community through your dashboard?

Whenever you elevate specific measures of progress, you are adjusting the incentives you offer to faculty and staff. Before agreeing to add any given measure of progress, reflect on how it will adjust the behavior of those charged with implementing a change. What are the unintended consequences of adding some measures relative to others? Weigh the risks of changing behavior in the way you intend against the risk of inducing undesirable, off-mission behaviors.

How is your dashboard balanced between quantitative and qualitative measures? Between objective and subjective assessments of progress?

Reflect to see if you have a set of concepts that will yield a balance between quantitative/qualitative and objective/subjective data once the dashboard is operationalized. Does that expected balance feel right, knowing your Board, parent, and faculty communities?

You will need an effective visual to help your leadership team and Board understand the design and potential impact of the dashboard. Here's a sample dashboard that might inspire what you'll create:

Figure 3. Strategic Dashboard for Board and Leadership

STRATEGIC VISION

MISSION

STRATEGIC CHOICE #1	STRATEGIC CHOICE #2	STRATEGIC CHOICE #3	STRATEGIC CHOICE #4	STRATEGIC CHOICE #5
Goal:	Goal:	Goal:	Goal:	Goal:
Goal:	Goal:	Goal:	Goal:	Goal:
Goal:	Goal:	Goal:	Goal:	Goal:
Goal:	Goal:	Goal:	Goal:	Goal:
Goal:	Goal:	Goal:	Goal:	Goal:

At Risk   Off Track

Return to Core Purpose: Affirm or Adapt Your Mission

Earlier, I suggested that you "back into mission." Now is the time to do so. The final step before adopting your strategy is to review your mission and see if it is aligned with your vision and your choices. Does the mission still hold? Or, given everything that you've learned, everything you've decided to do, and where you've decided to go, do you need to revise your mission for relevance and clarity?

Remember, your mission is your core purpose: it's what you do and why you exist. Your vision is your description of success in the future. Vision is the top of the mountain; mission is the reason why you are hiking in the first place. Reflecting on your mission can be an "aha moment" for schools that may have felt their mission statement was simply an obvious, even if beautifully written, statement that made them sound like every other school. I've found that schools often have mission statements that go well beyond statements into long narratives, blending mission, vision, values, and educational philosophy through lofty aspirational rhetoric. This is where you can seize the opportunity to get concise and clear about your purpose. You can distinguish mission from all the other elements that tend to be thrown into these statements and distill it to the purpose that matters most to you.

Sometimes, the reverse problem can be revealing. When I arrived at the Williston Northampton School, they had a crisp, clear mission statement: "We inspire our students to live with purpose, passion, and integrity." As we began our work, the Board questioned the mission. They were concerned about what it did not say: that the school was college preparatory, that it aspired to academic excellence, and so forth. As we went through the process of strategic design, we discovered that the mission statement was actually the galvanizing statement that brought students and faculty together with a sense of shared purpose. The school was indeed college preparatory and focused on excellence, but above all it valued the mission as stated. In the process of design, it affirmed its mission as its core purpose and used it more intentionally to make choices about what and how it would operate with respect to the educational program and the residential experience. Strategic design became an opportunity to double down on a mission that inspired learning and described the community and culture.

Securing a Commitment From the Board

The final milestone is to present your strategy and supporting materials to your Board for adoption. At this point your goal is to have the Board take ownership of the vision and plan in a very formal way. It is quite likely that you have been in constant contact with your Board, sharing drafts and soliciting input. By the time you go for their commitment, you should feel very confident in the language you've put forward in your one-page strategy (and that it is as active, distinctive, and clear as possible), the results you have tested (which point toward implementation), and your capacity to execute and assess progress. The Board should be asked to vote to adopt a final one-page strategy: the overarching vision for the future (your mission, vision, and core values of the school) and the key strategic choices. In the end, this will be translated into a public document for the school that the Board will endorse openly.

Your goal at the Board meeting is adoption on a technical level, but the real goal is for your Board members to walk away feeling fully informed of the internal and external factors you took into account as you formulated the one-page strategy while, of course, being completely delighted with the direction of the school. Trustees want to feel their own sense of shared purpose for the school; they want to feel optimistic about the future and confident in your leadership and your vision. Trustees also want to believe they can support and steward this vision, and that their investment of "time, talent, and treasure" will be valued and valuable. Your goal is to ensure that Trustees feel proud and empowered to take this strategy and use it to support the school in ways that advance their governance, as well as the health and the well-being of the institution. Inspire them to be your most articulate, informed, and influential ambassadors.

In my work, I am committed to involving Trustees in design so that they understand the strategy and are able to tell the stories that bring it to life. Engaged Trustees can draw a strong connection between their emotional feelings about the school and the logic of the plan. They are able to talk about the plan with anyone, anywhere, any time. Best of all, they have a strong sense of ownership for the design as a valid reflection of not only their work but the work of the entire community.

Sometimes, no matter how attentive you've been to including and updating Trustees, you may find yourself fielding opposing or differing views about elements of your design that seemed uncontroversial earlier. Occasionally, this is the moment when some Trustees engage even more deeply. If this happens, slow down and allow the dialogue to happen. This is a moment that needs your best facilitation expertise. There is the content of the decision or issue, but there is also the process for making the decision or resolving the tension. You need to attend to both. First, explore the content with everybody. What are we debating and how does it relate to our values? What are the important insights from your empathy interviews or from your reflections on the school's competitive landscape that drove your decision? Can you respectfully share how you anticipated the differing point of view that has surfaced in this discussion but chose the direction reflected in the one-page strategy?

Then there's a process for how you are going to make this decision. Being clear about which decisions belong to which parties is part of the process. For example, if you have a Board that has to make the decision and they're not sure, you might actually decide to put it to a vote. Or if it's a leadership team, maybe the Head of School has to make the ultimate decision. But be clear about who's making the decision, why, and how. Talking about decision making and understanding the process going forward is as important as the content of the decision itself.

This is a moment when an outside facilitator can help keep the process in motion. If opposing parties create a situation in which it is difficult to move forward, a good facilitator can get you unstuck and redirect the conversation back to your core values and vision. If you're stuck, chances are your values and your vision are not as clear as you thought they were. Members of your community may have significantly different interpretations of key words in your one-page strategy. If so, you need to get even clearer about them, and you need to have a process for decision making that's acceptable to the group.

Checklist #5: Adoption: Preparing a Final Document for the Board

◯ Define/confirm values

◯ Explain alignment of actions to values

◯ Identify key strategic choices

◯ Review initial test of values and vision (surveys, focus groups, and observations/learning walks)

◯ Update and include the Board/parents

◯ Share results of engaging the students as owners/designers

◯ Offer a protocol to facilitate the final drafting session

Notes:

LIVE YOUR STRATEGY: TIPS FOR GREAT EXECUTION

We don't learn from experience, we learn from reflecting on experience.

—John Dewey

Congratulations—you've done it! You've crafted a vision, designed a coherent approach shaped by a few clear choices, and are well on your way to becoming the school you aim to be now and in the future. It's time to celebrate your vision broadly and execute in earnest, using your design as a road map and guide. In the last chapter, I introduced tools for implementation so you could help others see the both the balcony and the dance floor in order to get comfortable with your design. Now you'll use those tools in earnest, if you haven't started already.

Our work with schools has revealed a series of key actions that help schools stay in the strategic thinking space, build leadership capacity, and check progress regularly. Remember, your success depends on the connections you build between your culture; your relentless work to execute; and your attention to your vision, values, and choices. I want you to stay at those intersections. It's easy to fall into the pattern of being busy and letting go of your larger vision, so here I'll share a few recommendations I've curated about the hard work of execution.

Resource Your Implementation Plan

Once you've received a commitment from the Board, the next phase is to map implementation and consider the implications for resource allocation. Your Board may be ready to go straight to work on critical decisions about how to allocate resources; budget; raise capital (through philanthropy or borrowing, or some other creative means); and how policy can be amended, streamlined, or adapted. An outline of your budgetary plans is sufficient at this stage. Less is more here—you want to stay agile!

Similarly, your faculty and staff now have clear parameters in which to work. They will be busy designing and executing and you may need to once again redirect talent toward the activities that are going to be most helpful to the school and the achievement of vision. Your biggest resources at school are your staff, which is already accounted for in your budget. However, there might be some call to action within the plan that requires budget focus: new hires, campus activities, or capital projects. Be intentional about identifying what pieces of the execution require resources or funding initiatives. Whether you need to assign people, recruit new expertise, or reallocate and raise funds, it's time to implement.

An implementation spreadsheet or software will help you anticipate and plan this work alongside the more tactical programmatic action steps you need to map. Generally speaking, you will partner at this stage with your Board's finance committee and your Chief Financial Officer, in coordination with the folks who are actually leading the charge of the implementation.

CUT COSTS IN ORDER TO REINVEST IN
WHAT MATTERS

Your design is meant to help you thrive. Cutting costs to
reduce overhead can be helpful, but I encourage you
to think equally hard about how you might reinvest and
redeploy money toward the capabilities you believe will
make you successful. Your finance committee and CFO

can use the one-page strategy to evaluate how to do
this and align it with the ways leadership, faculty, and
staff identify to work smarter rather than harder.

Build the Operating Culture You Need to Execute

A successful strategic design relies on and, in essence, describes the kind of culture you want. Building the culture you need to execute is critical and must be an early priority. I encourage you to make the strategic design process inclusive for this very reason: it signals what you hope to see inside your culture.

Early conversations among school leadership to explore what needs to be changed or cultivated are essential as you dive into execution. Return to your initial cultural inventory from Chapter 3 and the focus groups and learning walks from Chapter 6. Review your stop/start/continue feedback from Chapter 7. With this data in mind, identify a few key behaviors or dispositions you will need more of, and talk about how you expect the work to occur. Think about decision making, language choices around the narratives that shape how people think about the culture, and power dynamics.

> » How will you enable people to create and sustain the culture you want in your everyday work?

> » How will you ensure that decisions reflect the perspectives of the people who are impacted and/or closest to the work?

> » What needs to be made clear relative to your expectations, and what can be left open for people to create and innovate?

For example, your strategy may include a choice to foster more adult and student collaboration. Which aspects of the existing culture support that choice, and which obstacles or behaviors need to be removed so that you can clear up areas of confusion and people can get to work?

A second element of building culture goes back to the discussion from Chapter 2 regarding capacity. You'll build a culture that reflects and drives strategy if you cluster the right talent together in support of the priorities you've outlined. Organizations often try to spread their best people evenly across all functions, but some functions are more strategically critical than others. Be very clear about how you deploy staff. Invite them to collaborate powerfully on behalf of the entire system. In schools, if you get the right people in the right seats working well together, the culture follows.

Sometimes your strategy will offer the perfect context for making smart changes in organizational structure and function. You may need to recast your leadership team, or disband staid and unproductive committees that have lost relevance. You may wish to consolidate some activities or create temporary, project-focused teams to drive execution. The more agility you can build into your design, and the more growth, learning, and stretch you can offer to your best people, the faster you'll move. As a school leader, your engagement, support, and direction are critical. You'll want to ensure there are others around you rowing in the same direction.

You may wonder about the impact of organizational change, but don't be afraid of making the right changes—changes that signal your commitment to your vision and your strategic choices. Bold moves to align the organizational structure with the culture and functionality you want offer hope to the people who will push your new strategy forward. Yes, there will be those who are uncomfortable or resist the change. Embrace the discomfort as a signal of progress. Hear them, but don't allow their objections to make you tentative about moving forward. Engage them in solution building and remind them that resistance is not enough. Chances are these same people present resistance in other areas as well. It is more important is to give hope to the staff members who will shape your future than it is to appease those who oppose change and are unwilling to participate in creating new solutions.

Focus on People and Unleash Talented Teams

Building a culture depends on people who can help spread it. Strategic design is a wonderful opportunity to give people room to grow, explore their interests, and innovate and create in service of a shared purpose. One important outcome of this work will be the investment you make in the people who will actually bring your strategy to life and ensure its effective execution, so including them as designers is essential. It's also the related work you'll do to build culture and cluster talent where you need it most. A focus on people means you understand what each person brings to the table, and recognize where individual interests lie and what people need to thrive. With this context, you can cultivate conditions for success.

Focusing on people helps you build and ensure the capacity to execute well. It is important for two reasons. First, a focus on people—and their experience and involvement in the work—maximizes your possibility for success by ensuring you've matched talents to strategic needs. Second, it provides a clearer window into how to grow and develop your staff. Avoid tasking any significant initiative to only one individual. For your most urgent priorities you want to make sure that clusters of really strong people are collaborating effectively in service of your strategic choices. Teams are important to ensuring agile and smart execution. Somebody may need to be assigned ownership, but in the event that person goes away or gets redeployed, you need to ensure that there's enough breadth of ability to transfer ownership fairly easily within the team. I see too many programs or initiatives in schools that exist because of one person. That's simply not sustainable.

Finally, remember that in building culture and unleashing talent, you may have also clarified your organizational design, the leadership team, how decision making happens, how roles are defined, and how they relate to one another in service of strategy and mission. Without those elements, it's harder for people to know how to do their best work.

You can now move beyond leadership to empower people who are interested—faculty, staff, and even students—by assigning stretch opportunities or interesting work that develops their leadership and professional capacity. You've learned enough now to actually talk with your team about the nuts-and-bolts issues of implementation.

As mentioned earlier, you may decide to form flexible, project-focused teams. These small groups are based on the vision outlined in the one-page strategy, with each group working on a distinct priority. You might create a small working group of teachers and students to look at how they can incorporate service opportunities to their humanities curriculum. Another breakaway team can work on scheduling. A third might develop prototypes for programming.

Commit to Strategic Discipline

You are now probably noticing that building culture and executing strategy require the same discipline as the strategic design process. Execution is naturally decision-based—small and large decisions will shape how you move forward. Now is the time to use the filter of your one-page strategy. Don't stuff that design into a drawer! Your values and your vision are the first filter. Are the actions and decisions you make in alignment with your values and vision? If not, why not? Use the implementation plan and the scorecard, both shown in Chapter 8, as a mechanism for holding yourself attentive and accountable to alignment and follow through. If you're not regularly talking about and referring to the strategic design at every level of the work, the plan will get lost in the minutiae of the day-to-day business of school.

Broadcast your plan. Don't be bashful about pushing its significance in your school's future. Laminate it; post it everywhere; carry it on your mobile device, in your notebook or in your pocket. Identify the proper location and presence on your website: both the internal and external pages. Make it a part of your school's daily decision-making process. Schools that live their design refer to it unapologetically and in every context: students, parents, alumni, and faculty/staff share in it. It should become omnipresent.

With your design always on the radar, the dialogue can continue from the classroom to the boardroom and everywhere in between. Keep asking one another:

» How is what we are doing aligning with the vision and choices we've committed to in our design?

» What are the strengths we want to build on?

» What weaknesses can we address?

» What about the current experience must we understand or notice?

» Are we being relentless in our efforts to build capacities to support where we want to go and being equally attentive to what we must deprioritize?

NOTES: RECORD WHAT YOU LEARNED

Consider What Makes Good Execution Decisions

Decisions are often most successful when they consider the people they affect and the people who will carry them out. The hardest part of strategic design is moving from adoption of the conceptual plan to the reality of implementation. The more effective you are at involving your faculty, staff, and your students in this work, and in the decisions that affect them, the more likely you will win their commitment. It will help to have a checklist that helps you plan for implementation—the goals, action steps, and deliverables that help you enact strategy.

Checklist #6: Decision Making

- Who will consult to the team?

- Who will work together and communicate effectively to accomplish these goals?

- What tasks are essential?

- What are our respective milestones?

- What is our timeline?

- How will we ensure ongoing communication and feedback loops?

Execution can be overwhelming unless you break it into smaller chunks of activity. You may decide to do some preliminary action planning within your team as you steward your part of implementation. Sometimes it helps to map on paper some of the nitty-gritty details before you load it into your implementation or project management space. I really like the "MOCHA" model created by the Management Center (www. managementcenter.org/resources/assigning-responsibilities). Here's a sample action planning tool:

Action Planning Form

	1.	2.	3.	4.
ACTION STEPS				
OBJECTIVE (WHY)				
PEOPLE (WHO)				
PREPARATION AND PROCESS (HOW)				
LOGISTICS (WHERE AND WHEN)				
COMMUNICATIONS (WHY, WHERE, WHEN, HOW, AND WHAT)				
TECH AND TOOLS				
OWNER (ULTIMATE ACCOUNTABILITY)				
STATUS/NOTES				

You've designed a strategy that integrates the many activities of your school. Now let's allow your people to do the same. Bring questions like these to your teams:

» **How** can our organization continue to evolve in ways that find answers at the intersections, rather than within separate departments or functional areas?

» **How** can we balance our need for agency, creativity, and risk-taking in learning with our need to comply and manage institutional risk at the system level?

» **How** can we create space for people to work across and transcend their functional boundaries?

» **How** can people in advancement and admissions partner with teachers on execution challenges?

» **How** can science teachers work with arts faculty to design new experiences for students?

NOTES: RECORD WHAT YOU LEARNED

Move From Static to Active

Change takes time. You won't discover answers right away, and you'll probably not be able to tackle all your strategic choices at once. Keep utilizing your new design-thinking skills and continue to test prototypes in small ways so that you begin to get a clearer vision of what you have to do in the long term to fully transform your school. You'll gain experience, reflect on the experience, and move toward your vision step-by-step. The key to implementation work is to stay in what I call the "active" part of strategy. Your one-page strategy on paper is "static," but your living process of try, test, and reflect is "active."

Let's say your vision states that you will create an environment in which students consistently engage in meaningful, real-world projects and problems in order to deepen their learning. You may decide that one of your early execution goals is to free up time in your calendar schedule for these projects so students can move out into the community and interact with other professionals. In your strategic choices, or in the underlying goals, you might have stated that you will change the schedule. Now you move into the "active" stage in which you allow people to start doing the work. You can start with a schedule prototype. These don't have to be permanent: you can take time to implement smaller-scale and temporary changes and "build the plane as you fly it" by soliciting

Creating Schools That Thrive: A Blueprint for Strategy

feedback, and trusting and empowering faculty to work with students to change how they use time together. Give yourself a semester so you can really see how it all works. Then you can reflect and begin to spread and implement deeper changes to the master schedule going forward.

Remember, your one-page strategy is a working guide—a means, not an end. You created your strategy with the recognition that you operate in an environment that may change or be unpredictable. Your design does not prescribe a sequence of clearly defined steps guaranteed to get you there. But it does give you a North Star, and a tool to apply as you adapt, learn, and make choices. It is a work in progress. Consult it, build with it, and consistently communicate it as you progress.

Know What Makes Schools Dynamic

So much of what educators are used to doing in schools actually reinforces what is "static" in nature. But the key to a successful strategic design is shifting your focus to what is active rather than static. This will help you operate dynamically and drive impact. Focus first on implementing elements of your plan in an active way and then design the "static" supports to structure and sustain the work. Resist the temptation to immediately jump into writing policies, mapping curriculum scope and sequence, publishing handbooks, and other efforts to develop static structures that can take years to be approved and, in the meantime, make no immediate impact. You'll only exhaust and depress your resources, and change nothing for your students.

For example, you'll get much more return on your efforts if you focus on pedagogy over curriculum. Pedagogy is a core dynamic of learning—it's where the real levers for change exist. By working on pedagogical practices, supporting your staff as they test and try new approaches to learning, and offering lots of feedback and opportunity for reflection with other adults and students, you can immediately assess impact inside and outside your classrooms. To execute effectively, focus on the elements in the right-hand column.

STATIC

Fixed and/or prescriptive in nature; often used to ensure outcomes but instead bar change and creativity. Less responsive to human needs.

ACTIVE

Meaningful and "real-time" ways to effect change and produce outcomes. More human centered.

CURRICULA AND STANDARDS

PEDAGOGY AND ASSESSMENT

DIVERSITY TARGETS

INCLUSIVE PRACTICES

ORGANIZATIONAL STRUCTURE

TEAMS AND CROSS-FUNCTIONAL DESIGN

POLICIES AND PROCEDURES

COMMUNICATION AND COLLABORATION

Start with the Low-Hanging Fruit

Addressing low-hanging fruit—the changes that can be easily implemented—is so satisfying! The best part is that as you conquer each task, you gain momentum and energy. And, you may discover another layer of low-hanging fruit that can be tackled just to sustain momentum.

Often, low-hanging fruit, if picked, can have immediate impact on school climate, which is a lot easier to change than its culture. For example, small things like aesthetics—paint, furniture, student work on the walls and in classrooms, landscaping—can make big differences in how everyone feels about their environment. Similarly, small tweaks in practice—assessments, community gatherings, approaches to discipline, or dorm life—can instantly help strengthen the bonds of community.

Fortunately, low-hanging fruit is usually easy to spot in the results of your "stop/start/continue" reflections from Chapter 7. Go back to that and make some quick decisions. Some low-hanging fruit might also include easy suggestions to test and prototype. Don't shy away from these projects even if they feel small to you. Adjustments in the new practices teachers or students use in the classroom may be a smaller piece of the strategic puzzle, but they will feel vital to those who execute them. They will be energized by the support or encouragement for their ideas and your commitment to allowing them to be brought to life. This can create a stronger connection between leadership and staff to take on the larger strategic initiative you have in mind.

The reason I recommend starting with the low-hanging fruit is that the underlying goal is to build momentum. You want to test things that will fuel optimism and a sense of confidence. For example, let's say that you want to develop students' ability to manage stress and their emotions. You might have classroom teachers trying mindfulness exercises in an advisory or homeroom setting, and then have these same teachers introduce this work to the rest of the teaching staff. A spreadable practice like this would be considered low-hanging fruit because it is easy to implement and costs nothing. Teachers can report back how the exercise session went, and then decide as a team how they might integrate this in a deeper way.

Keep Your Design Fresh with Feedback and Assessment

Keep reviewing the action steps you are taking toward your incremental goals. You'll get some things right and others will miss the mark. That's okay! Learn, adjust, and update your implementation plan by recalibrating regularly. As you learn, talk about it, document and measure, and clearly communicate the why and what of your adjustments. Make sure you meet regularly to update your implementation plan and reflect on your learning so you continue to be nimble, responsive, and focused.

Measure What Matters Most

Once you are in the thick of implementation, it's easy to get focused on activities and what people are doing every day. This is necessary but not sufficient. The key to being strategic is to connect people's actions to outcomes. This is where your dashboard will be most effective: to evaluate the success of your strategic design and the its execution.

Ensure that the steps you are taking link back to your vision and are measurable using your dashboard. Make sure this connection is explicit: talk about it with your team, faculty, and staff and remind them that at the heart of what they do is the student experience and your identified outcomes. Establish early in the implementation process that all prototyping and testing should be coupled with a measurement protocol and a responsibility to communicate results to the members of the leadership team, who serve as custodians of the dashboard.

As you saw in Chapter 8, you can measure process and outcomes, quality and quantity (e.g., growth, frequency, experience). You can monitor with timelines, milestones, and deliverables. As you start to execute improvements in student experience and institutional performance, revisit what you will track and reach consensus about the forms of measurement you will select, collect, and rely upon in the short and medium term.

Achieving clarity and consensus about operationalization is essential to your ability to later declare with confidence your success in achieving the plan. Few moments in strategic planning and execution are more dispiriting than disputes about measurement. Uncertainty about how exactly you will know if you are succeeding can quickly undermine motivation to take on the hard work involved in implementing changes in practice.

Lastly, determine how, when, where, and with whom you'll report your results. Although the discussions of how to operationalize key dashboard measures will likely be composed of a smaller group within the leadership team, expand the conversation about reporting to include both the school leadership team and the Board leadership. Ensuring that the Board fully embraces the reporting strategy and approach to sharing data will allow you to appear unified to your community as you carry out your dual roles of execution and oversight.

Checklist #7: Measuring Performance

- What is the available testing data?

- What are the available survey questions?

- What new testing, surveys, focus groups, or observational protocols do you need to create?

- Which of the various ways to operationalize match up to the goals or changes we are initiating?

Lean Into Your Board

Your Board will continue to play a critical role in the execution of your strategic design. Trustees will ask for information and want to track your progress. Your implementation plan and dashboard provide the data you need to illustrate how you are charting your course and what you are learning. Don't panic—it's not about the Board "getting down on the dance floor" but rather about involving Trustees as informed strategists so they can support and troubleshoot effectively from the balcony. You want them to hold your vision, protect your values, and be future focused so they can anticipate and create conditions for success.

It's important to help the Board think about how they will work as a governance body and with the rest of the school relative to the plan. It makes sense to align Board work with the strategic design. As Board members develop their goals and agendas for what they want to focus on, don't hesitate to ask them what they need or what they'd like to change about how they work. Partner with your Board Chair and committee heads to talk about how governance practice will evolve. Help them integrate their work with your execution of strategy.

One helpful step is to set up a reporting schedule so that they can build an agenda that allows them to support you effectively. Share your feedback, your trouble spots, and your success stories so that they feel comfortable that you are being transparent. Trustees are smart; they know execution is hard work. I've been told countless times by Trustees, "I wish I knew what keeps him/her [the Head of School] up at night." Don't shy away from creating this deeper strategic partnership. I have found time and again that the strategic design process changes Board dynamics and governance function for the better. It often makes your Board stronger, and frankly, it makes your Trustees feel a lot more valued and engaged.

Sustain Focus and Energy: Stay Nimble by Being Strategic

If I've learned one thing from my clients, it is that conditions in and around their schools are always changing. The best way you can respond to change is to stay in the strategic mindset. The trap that schools fall into is that they do strategic planning and then they stop and "regress to the mean" of standard operating practice. Then, they lift themselves up for a few months once again in five or seven years. If that's you, escape this cycle now. It is error number one. Take what you've learned through this process and use it every day going forward.

At this point you can allow the strategic design committee to disband, and reimagine a new group that can act as a strategic oversight or strategic issues committee. This can include a couple of Trustees in coordination with the Head of School and other school leadership team members as you see fit. Their responsibility will be to continue to focus on anticipating strategic needs and helping with the oversight of the plan. This is typically a smaller committee that can expand only when necessary. This committee should have the clear charge to facilitate strategic dialogue, oversight, and learning at the Board level and with school leadership.

For instance, I served on the Board at an independent day school in my community. We formed a committee called the Learning Committee to identify and explore strategic issues and questions. The committee's purpose is to continually learn in order to stay engaged, informed, and generative in Board work. It brings issues to the table and relates them to strategic goals, looking for ways to inform future thinking.

Case Study: Germantown Academy

Germantown Academy is a wonderful example of a school that wanted to reimagine how it did strategic planning. When I got the call in 2014 from the Head of School, Jim Connor, we abandoned the notion of the old, traditional strategic planning process and worked directly with the Board over the course of three years. About halfway through, we were able to articulate a very bold and exciting strategic vision, but we never actually created a traditional strategic plan. Instead, Germantown Academy does strategic design all the time by aligning goals to their vision and continually reflecting on their progress and learning.

We focused on their vision of deep engagement to drive the work and jump straight into execution. We also used their vision as away to coordinate and/or edit the various innovative activities and pilot programs that were already going on at the school. We continue to work with the school, particularly with the Board, to assess where they are relative to their vision, and to help the Board establish its own goals in coordination with the goals of the leadership team. From that vision, we look at "engagement" as its core purpose. We uncovered what an engaged learner, educator, and even Trustee look like, and then developed programs and assessments that measured engagement. These decisions had implications for programs and assessments for teachers, how they would be hired in the future, and how they were supported and developed. It had implications for how the Board operates, sets agendas, provides oversight, and conducts and structures itself.

In the midst of all of our collaboration, there was a leadership transition that we were able to carefully manage, and plan in concert with the development of this strategic vision. The vision was developed by the outgoing Head in partnership with the incoming, and we were able to create a sense of forward motion and continuity even as we transitioned into new leadership.

Don't Stop Communicating Externally

After you've celebrated your new design and moved deep into execution, people may need to be reminded why you are making changes, or how your actions relate back to your design. This is one reason why you want your one-page strategy to be omnipresent. But that is still not enough. Please don't assume that everybody in your community is as up to speed as you are about how certain actions or decisions relate back to the design. Be intentional about explaining how it works. Remember, your strategic design was a process that helped you articulate and commit to a clear vision. Help your whole community understand that vision by continuing to talk about it in relation to both your balcony and dance floor decisions. Give them opportunities to participate in and take ownership of this vision. You cannot overcommunicate, overconnect, or be too repetitive. We know from the research that people have to hear about what you do, experience it, and take it in in order to understand and integrate it effectively.

Your strategic design will continue to be the core of your narrative even as it evolves. One of the ways that you can communicate effectively with the larger community is to share your successes, which give evidence of why your plan matters and how your plan is working. You can share these success stories in all sorts of media. Write letters that showcase students and teachers, or craft press releases or magazine articles about community events. Use video to create a story that highlights how new traditions or ceremonies showcase your values, and post it on your website or distribute to your email lists. Talk about something that's happening in a particular classroom, or in a particular program, that is evidence of your plan. Push these stories out with regularity so the community feels connected to what's happening at school. Whatever vehicle you choose, use stories to showcase how your plan comes to life and why it matters.

Communication is critical to culture and community building, but it is equally important to advancement, admissions, master planning, and other essential activities that help you develop resources and advance your mission. The more you communicate, the easier it is for every single member of your community to speak about your institution effectively and participate in all that you create. And frankly, that's critical to your ability to thrive as a living ecosystem for learners. All of your stakeholders need to understand why your school matters, what's important about you, and how you do what you do. If you're communicating clearly and consistently through multiple channels, the distinctive essence of your school becomes evident to everyone in your community. That makes it easier when it comes time to support you or choose you as an institution.

Good Luck!

My hope is that you came to strategic design because it's time to do strategic planning at your school. Now that you have gone through the process, you won't need to return to this cycle. I hope this book encourages you to transform into a school that is living strategic design all the time. The next time you sense that there is room for growth or change, the process will be less about forming committees and more about doing what's right in the moment.

There still may be times when you have a formal strategic planning cycle: for example, you may want to elevate the visibility of the work process, perhaps to coincide with a development initiative. But the point of this book is that strategic thinking and design should happen every day. You should always be involved in a process that encompasses an intentional and widespread approach to listen and learn from constituents across your school community. Now that you are a strategically nimble organization, you can continuously harness the mindsets and tools of strategy. Onward!

Notes:

CPSIA information can be obtained
at www.ICGtesting.com
Printed in the USA
FSHW02n1528140618
49326FS